CliffsNotes™

Stowe's
Uncle Tom's Cabin

By Mary Patterson Thornburg, Ph.D.

IN THIS BOOK

- Learn about the Life and Background of the Author
- Preview an Introduction to the Novel
- Study a graphical Character Map
- Explore themes and literary devices in the Critical Commentaries
- Examine in-depth Character Analyses
- Enhance your understanding of the work with Critical Essays
- Reinforce what you learn with CliffsNotes Review
- Find additional information to further your study in CliffsNotes Resource Center and online at www.cliffsnotes.com

IDG Books Worldwide, Inc.
An International Data Group Company
Foster City, CA • Chicago, IL • Indianapolis, IN • New York, NY

About the Author

Mary Patterson Thornburg attended Holy Names College, Spokane, WA, and took her undergraduate degree from Montana State University. She holds the M.A. and Ph.D. from Ball State University, where she taught English until 1998; she lives with her husband, Thomas Thornburg, in Montana.

Publisher's Acknowledgments
Editorial
Project Editor: Tracy Barr
Acquisitions Editor: Greg Tubach
Glossary Editors: The editors and staff at Webster's New World™ Dictionaries
Editorial Administrator: Michelle Hacker
Production
Indexer: York Production Services, Inc.
Proofreader: York Production Services, Inc.
IDG Books Indianapolis Production Department

CliffsNotes™ Stowe's *Uncle Tom's Cabin*
Published by
IDG Books Worldwide, Inc.
An International Data Group Company
919 E. Hillsdale Blvd.
Suite 400
Foster City, CA 94404
www.idgbooks.com (IDG Books Worldwide Web site)
www.cliffsnotes.com (CliffsNotes Web site)

Note: If you purchased this book without a cover, you should be aware that this book is stolen property. It was reported as "unsold and destroyed" to the publisher, and neither the author nor the publisher has received any payment for this "stripped book."

Library of Congress Control Number: 00-107793

ISBN: 0-7645-8677-7

Printed in the United States of America

10 9 8 7 6 5 4 3 2 1

1O/QU/RS/QQ/IN

Distributed in the United States by IDG Books Worldwide, Inc.

Distributed by CDG Books Canada Inc. for Canada; by Transworld Publishers Limited in the United Kingdom; by IDG Norge Books for Norway; by IDG Sweden Books for Sweden; by IDG Books Australia Publishing Corporation Pty. Ltd. for Australia and New Zealand; by TransQuest Publishers Pte Ltd. for Singapore, Malaysia, Thailand, Indonesia, and Hong Kong; by Gotop Information Inc. for Taiwan; by ICG Muse, Inc. for Japan; by Norma Comunicaciones S.A. for Columbia; by Intersoft for South Africa; by Eyrolles for France; by International Thomson Publishing for Germany, Austria and Switzerland; by Distribuidora Cuspide for Argentina; by LR International for Brazil; by Galileo Libros for Chile; by Ediciones ZETA S.C.R. Ltda. for Peru; by WS Computer Publishing Corporation, Inc., for the Philippines; by Contemporanea de Ediciones for Venezuela; by Express Computer Distributors for the Caribbean and West Indies; by Micronesia Media Distributor, Inc. for Micronesia; by Grupo Editorial Norma S.A. for Guatemala; by Chips Computadoras S.A. de C.V. for Mexico; by Editorial Norma de Panama S.A. for Panama; by American Bookshops for Finland. Authorized Sales Agent: Anthony Rudkin Associates for the Middle East and North Africa.

For general information on IDG Books Worldwide's books in the U.S., please call our Consumer Customer Service department at 800-762-2974. For reseller information, including discounts and premium sales, please call our Reseller Customer Service department at 800-434-3422.

For information on where to purchase IDG Books Worldwide's books outside the U.S., please contact our International Sales department at 317-572-3993 or fax 317-572-4002.

For consumer information on foreign language translations, please contact our Customer Service department at 1-800-434-3422, fax 317-572-4002, or e-mail rights@idgbooks.com.

For information on licensing foreign or domestic rights, please phone +1-650-653-7098.

For sales inquiries and special prices for bulk quantities, please contact our Order Services department at 800-434-3422 or write to the address above.

For information on using IDG Books Worldwide's books in the classroom or for ordering examination copies, please contact our Educational Sales department at 800-434-2086 or fax 317-572-4005.

For press review copies, author interviews, or other publicity information, please contact our Public Relations department at 650-653-7000 or fax 650-653-7500.

For authorization to photocopy items for corporate, personal, or educational use, please contact Copyright Clearance Center, 222 Rosewood Drive, Danvers, MA 01923, or fax 978-750-4470.

 is a registered trademark under exclusive license to IDG Books Worldwide, Inc. from International Data Group, Inc.

Table of Contents

How to Use This Book

CliffsNotes Stowe's *Uncle Tom's Cabin* supplements the original work, giving you background information about the author, an introduction to the novel, a graphical character map, critical commentaries, expanded glossaries, and a comprehensive index. CliffsNotes Review tests your comprehension of the original text and reinforces learning with questions and answers, practice projects, and more. For further information on Harriet Beecher Stowe and *Uncle Tom's Cabin*, check out the CliffsNotes Resource Center.

CliffsNotes provides the following icons to highlight essential elements of particular interest:

Reveals the underlying themes in the work.

Helps you to more easily relate to or discover the depth of a character.

Uncovers elements such as setting, atmosphere, mystery, passion, violence, irony, symbolism, tragedy, foreshadowing, and satire.

Enables you to appreciate the nuances of words and phrases.

Don't Miss Our Web Site

Discover classic literature as well as modern-day treasures by visiting the Cliffs Notes Web site at www.cliffsnotes.com. You can obtain a quick download of a CliffsNotes title, purchase a title in print form, browse our catalog, or view online samples.

You'll also find interactive tools that are fun and informative, links to interesting Web sites, tips, articles, and additional resources to help you, not only for literature, but for test prep, finance, careers, computers, and the Internet too. See you at www.cliffsnotes.com!

LIFE AND BACKGROUND OF THE AUTHOR

Early Years and Education

Harriet Beecher was born in Litchfield, Connecticut, on June 13, 1811. She was the seventh of nine children born to Roxana Foote Beecher, the granddaughter of a Revolutionary general, and Lyman Beecher, a blacksmith's son and Congregational minister. Her mother died when Harriet was five years old, and her father remarried a year later; her stepmother would give birth to four more children. Harriet often visited at the home of her widowed maternal grandmother and unmarried aunt, who instructed her in religion and taught her needlework. Her mother and aunts, although necessarily practiced in domestic skills like spinning and weaving, had also been unusually well educated for young women of their time, and Harriet's early association with the Foote family probably contributed not only to the intellectual curiosity she would have all her life, but also to her confidence that she could combine a career as writer with that of housewife and mother.

At the age of six, Harriet entered primary school and two years later was enrolled in the Litchfield Female Academy. She seems in some ways to have been a rather odd little girl, bright and talented in her schoolwork but also full of mischief, shy but at the same time hungry for attention. Fortunately, her father was proud of her intelligence and imagination. He encouraged her progress in school; indeed, he was to be supportive of her all his life, and the entire Beecher family was to remain close. At thirteen, after listening to one of her father's sermons, Harriet experienced a personal "conversion" and committed herself to Christianity, a commitment she would renew throughout her life.

At about the same age, Harriet moved to the larger city of Hartford, Connecticut, and entered the Hartford Female Seminary, a private secondary school founded a few years earlier by her older sister Catharine Beecher. Harriet was to remain until she was 21, first as a student and, from 1827 to 1832, as a teacher. One of the first American schools for women, the seminary featured classes in many traditional male school subjects such as grammar, composition, English literature, logic, rhetoric and oratory, Latin, and ethics, as well as French, Italian, drawing, and music. Catharine also emphasized the sciences, which she believed were slighted in women's education; her pupils' studies included chemistry, "natural philosophy" (what we would probably call "earth science"), geometry, and astronomy. They also studied geography, and in her last year at the Hartford school, Harriet wrote and published a geography textbook that would remain in print for some years and be adopted by numerous schools.

Early Writing and Marriage

Harriet's first non-academic writing was in letters through which she attempted to express her feelings and beliefs clearly and movingly. Another vehicle for writing, slightly more public, was the unofficial school newspaper, which Harriet edited briefly when she was 14 and for which she wrote frequently. The paper's subjects were mostly playful and humorous or satirical, giving her practice at the irony that would mark the best of her adult writing.

In 1832, Harriet's father moved to Cincinnati, Ohio, to head Lane Seminary. Harriet, Catharine, and four more of their siblings traveled with him and his wife by stagecoach. Harriet, just turned 21, would spend her next 18 years in Cincinnati. Within a short while of her arrival in Cincinnati, Harriet was invited to join a social and literary club (the "Semicolons"), an informal group whose members gathered to read aloud from each other's contributions, mostly short, lighthearted, often satirical prose sketches and essays or verse. In this production of what her biographer Joan D. Hedrick calls "parlor literature," Harriet continued to shape herself as a writer.

Among the other members of the "Semicolons" were a young biblical scholar and professor, Calvin Stowe, and his wife Eliza. Eliza and Harriet became close friends. But in August of 1834, while Harriet was visiting relatives in the East, Eliza Stowe died of cholera. Within eight months of his wife's death, Calvin proposed to Harriet, and they were married in January of 1836. In September of that year, Harriet gave birth to twin girls, and sixteen months later to a baby boy. In all, she was to have seven children (and numerous miscarriages) between 1836 and 1850. Her second-to-last child, baby Charley, would die in 1849 at 18 months of cholera. Although hardly an unusual event for the time when infant mortality was still very high, Harriet and her husband suffered intense grief, and this loss would be reflected two years later in the writing of *Uncle Tom's Cabin*, both in the famous death scene of the saintly child Eva and in the author's identification throughout the novel with parents whose children were taken forcibly from them by the terrible system of slavery.

By 1837, Harriet's geography textbook had sold widely to schools, and she saw that writing could supplement her husband's income. Beginning even before her marriage, Harriet published short fiction in popular magazines and church periodicals, and in 1843, Harper Brothers publishers brought out *The Mayflower*, a collection of her stories and sketches. She also wrote religious pamphlets and essays in literary criticism.

Less than a year after the death of her sixth child, pregnant with her seventh, Harriet left Cincinnati for Brunswick, Maine, where her husband had accepted a teaching post. She had written very little for five years and had never attempted a long work of fiction, but now she was about to begin the book that would make her famous and would influence antislavery sentiment not only in the United States but around the world as well.

Stowe's Masterpiece and Other Works

Harriet's family and friends had been involved in antislavery activities in Cincinnati, where there was fierce debate (and some violence) not only between pro- and antislavery activists but also among antislavery factions. At least one of Harriet's brothers was a radical abolitionist, while other Beechers, her father among them, were "colonizationists," favoring a "gradual" approach to freeing slaves, who would then be returned to African colonies. Harriet seems to have agreed, at least partly, with the latter view, but she became more radical at the beginning of the 1850s. In part, this may have been because of her child's death and her anxious attachment to the baby born a year later. The inhumanity of a system that separated parents from their children without recourse must have struck her as never before through this event in her personal life. At about the same time, Congress passed a Fugitive Slave Law, requiring that people who had escaped from slavery into the free states of the North be returned to captivity. This latest federal compromise with the slaveholding states of the South, along with Harriet's personal loss, seems to have energized her creatively, and when the editor of the antislavery periodical *The National Era* invited her to write something for his journal, she began to send him installments of *Uncle Tom's Cabin*.

The story, which turned out to be much longer than Harriet had expected, was published in book form in 1852 and immediately became a bestseller. As its popularity soared, it inspired songs, dramatizations, prints, and paintings. Harriet was soon threatened with a lawsuit by a Philadelphia clergyman whose defense of slavery she had quoted, accurately enough, in the book. The suit was never brought, but the uproar it caused in the press prompted Harriet, helped by family and friends, to collect damning evidence from court records, newspaper accounts, and other sources to support her published allegations about slavery. What she discovered was more horrifying than she had anticipated, refuting the claims of Southern critics that the fictional incidents in

Uncle Tom's Cabin were based on invention or exaggeration. Harriet selected and published the results of her research in 1853, in the 259-page book *A Key to Uncle Tom's Cabin*.

Harriet continued to write for publication until 1878. Her non-fiction (or semi-fictional) works, including sketches and essays with fictional narrators, mostly written for various periodicals, were eventually collected in book form as *Sunny Memories of Foreign Lands* (1854); *Household Papers and Stories* (1865–67, 1896); *Little Foxes* (1866); *Palmetto Leaves* (1873); *Women in Sacred History* (1874); and *Footsteps of the Master* (1877).

Her long fiction after *Uncle Tom's Cabin* is uneven in quality. Both *Dred: A Tale of the Great Dismal Swamp* (1856, written during the violent period following passage of the Kansas-Nebraska Act) and *The Pearl of Orr's Island* (1862) start strongly but weaken toward the end, while *Agnes of Sorrento* (1862), set in a romanticized Italy, is relatively shapeless and shallow. *Oldtown Folks* (1869), which Harriet hoped would be her masterpiece, suffered from domestic distractions she endured while attempting to finish it, including the necessity to find adequate care for her son Fred, a struggling alcoholic. *My Wife and I* and *Pink and White Tyranny*, both published as magazine serials in 1871, are fictional criticisms of contemporary figures and ideas in the women's rights movement. Her last work, *Poganuk People* (1878), written when Harriet was in her late sixties, is more successful, probably because in writing it she felt not only less pressure to make a specific political or moral statement but also less pressure to complete the work in a specific length of time.

Harriet's most controversial publication came in 1869, with "The True Story of Lady Byron's Life," published in *Atlantic Monthly*, in which she revealed the scandalous "secret" (actually fairly well known in private circles) of the famous English poet's brief marriage and notorious separation from his wife. The uproar caused by this article prompted her to write *Lady Byron Vindicated* (1870), which she hoped would support the *Atlantic* article (as *A Key to Uncle Tom's Cabin* had done for her famous and controversial novel) but which was itself vilified and ridiculed.

After 1878, Harriet virtually retired from writing except for letters. Her husband died in 1886, her daughter Georgiana the next year. Of her six children who had lived to adulthood, only her twin daughters, Hattie and Eliza, and her youngest child, called Charley like the dead infant, survived her. They were with her when she died in 1896 at 85.

Harriet Beecher Stowe was a writer from youth to old age, encouraged by her family and sustained by the conviction that she could accomplish social and moral good in this way, just as her father, husband, and brothers could by preaching and teaching. More than a century after her death, she is remembered almost solely for *Uncle Tom's Cabin*, the novel that forced white readers to identify and sympathize with the Africans and African Americans enslaved in the Southern United States. Today, it is difficult to realize the electrifying power of this book when it first appeared. It is easy to find fault with the overwhelming sentimentality of Little Eva's death scene, which affected nineteenth-century readers much differently than it does us; with the condescending characterization of some of the slaves; and especially with the sweet Christian passivity of Uncle Tom himself, whose behavior is the antithesis of what our own age finds admirable. Still, *Uncle Tom's Cabin* remains arguably the most important work of fiction ever published in the United States: a bold moral statement by a woman in a day when women were expected to be silent, and an unabashed portrait of American life in a day when American literature was still in the process of defining itself. Above all, it was a book that swayed its millions of readers into opposition to the monstrous institution of slavery, whose roots were buried in the earliest days of the nation and whose consequences extend into our own time.

INTRODUCTION TO THE NOVEL

Introduction

In 1851, after the enactment by the United States Congress of a Fugitive Slave Act (the effect of which was to return Africans and African Americans who had escaped from slavery in the Southern states and were living in the North, back into captivity), the editor of an anti-slavery periodical asked Harriet Beecher Stowe if she could supply him with a timely story or article. Stowe agreed to write a fictional piece about the lives of several slaves on a Kentucky plantation. It was a subject she knew a little about, having visited such a plantation briefly and having talked and corresponded with people who had a more detailed knowledge; moreover, it was a subject that moved her deeply. She expected that her story, printed in serial form, would run for three or four installments. In fact, it would turn out to be much longer and would require some hurried research, as Stowe's characters took her into places and situations of which she had little or no knowledge.

The story, as it ran, was immensely popular, and when it was published in book form in 1852, it immediately became a runaway bestseller in both the U.S. and Great Britain. The effect of this emotionally powerful book was to galvanize public opinion against slavery in a way that no strictly moral or intellectual argument had as yet been able to accomplish. President Lincoln supposedly said, upon meeting Stowe in 1862, "So you're the little woman who wrote the book that caused this great war." In a very real sense, he was right.

Uncle Tom's Cabin was first of all a popular book, effective because people identified with its sympathetic characters and thrilled to its incidents. Readers of all ages and levels of education, male and female, American and British, black and white (although the book was certainly intended chiefly for a white audience), made *Uncle Tom's Cabin* one of the most successful bestsellers to be published in the United States. And whether or not the average nineteenth-century reader agreed with the book, he or she had no trouble recognizing and understanding its language, assumptions, and fictional conventions. However, that is not the case with the average reader today. Stowe's novel presents modern readers with several problems that bear examination.

The first problem, ironically, is the book's reputation brought about by its early popularity. Dramatic versions over which Stowe had little or no control (and for which she received few or no royalties) appeared within months of its publication, and it is probably no exaggeration to say that *Uncle Tom's Cabin*, in one stage version or another, was one of the most frequently produced plays of the next half-century. Thus it was eventually better "known" from its dramatizations, which often departed wildly from the actual novel, than from the book itself. The stereotypical "Uncle Tom," a gentle, white-haired old man; the comic Topsy, all pigtails and rolling eyes; syrupy-sweet and saintly Eva—these are the characters we remember, if we remember the story at all, and we may dread having to encounter them in the pages of the novel. Luckily, they are not Stowe's characters, as readers may be surprised to learn. The problem of the "Uncle Tom" stereotypes is soon overcome when we actually read the book.

A second problem, one with a real basis in the book, might be called one of "political correctness." There are probably very few white Americans, if the truth were known, who do not harbor some prejudiced (or, put less kindly, racist) ideas about black people, and especially about African Americans. This was no doubt equally true in the 1850s, although the ideas may have been different. We all tend to be so conscious today of this prejudiced condition (if not always of the nature of the prejudices) that most white writers would think it foolhardy to attempt a novel whose central characters are African Americans and would certainly not undertake to explain to readers the nature of the "African race."

Such considerations did not occur to Harriet Beecher Stowe. Not only does she use language (for example, *negro*—and sometimes *negress*—with a small *n*) that was polite in her time but is not in ours, and not only do her characters, even some of the sympathetic ones, say *nigger* all too frequently, but Stowe in her role as narrator often takes time out to tell her readers what black people are like: They are home-loving rather than adventurous, for example; they have admirable but highly exotic taste in clothing and décor; and, of course, they generally have simple, childish hearts. The fact that Stowe does not repeat, and obviously does not believe, the more repellent stereotypes, and the fact that her African and African-American characters often behave in ways quite counter to her explanations, will not save her from being sneered at by twenty-first-century readers. Nor will the fact that she meant well; but we must offer that as one defense of her political incorrectness, another being that she lived in a less enlightened time, a third being that an examination of the errors she fell into might help lead us to recognize and correct our own.

Fashions in racial thinking and speaking are not the only ones that have changed since 1852. A third problem with *Uncle Tom's Cabin* for the modern reader is its sentimentality, which we may use as a sort of blanket term for the novel's literary style. In several ways, Stowe's book follows the models of Charles Dickens, with its two main plots, its several imbedded narratives, its grotesque and comic characters, its pairs of happy and unhappy lovers. Perhaps because Stowe (again like Dickens, often) not only published but also wrote the book in installments, the plots tend to wander and to be tied up eventually by a set of scarcely believable coincidences. The descriptions tend to be long: readers had more patience in 1852 than we do and less available visual entertainment. Above all, Stowe interjects her narrator's voice, speaking directly to the reader, far more often than we might like. To a student of the nineteenth-century sentimental novel, *Uncle Tom's Cabin* is, if anything, much less tedious than might be expected. But readers not used to these conventions should try to bear with them, suspend disbelief in some instances, and finally relax and enjoy Stowe's dry, often understated, ironic wit.

Finally, Stowe's Christianity may present a problem for some readers. The daughter, sister, and wife of Protestant clergymen and a committed Christian herself, the writer lived at a time when many Americans assumed that the United States was "a Christian country"— and a Protestant country at that. To *educate* a person, in Stowe's usage, was to *make a Christian* of him or her, and she does not apologize for her Protestant chauvinism. (At one point in the book, a character makes a slurring remark about "the Jews"; and one can almost feel the forbearance with which Stowe allows some of her New Orleans characters to be Roman Catholics, a sect about whose liturgy she obviously knows next to nothing.) One of the book's major themes is the culpability of Christian churches, North and South, in countenancing slavery, and an even more pronounced theme is that of Christianity itself. Uncle Tom, the central character, is above all a Christian. His trials and sufferings are not so much those of an African in America, nor of a slave, nor of a husband and father separated from his family, as they are of a man attempting to follow Christ's life and teachings; his victory is not a victory of nature but of grace. In our secular time, we tend to avoid the discussion of religion in ordinary "non-religious" circumstances. The separation of Church and State, however, meant something quite different to Stowe, and in reading her book, we will do well to accept, at least for that time, her religious premises and assumptions.

A Brief Synopsis

Arthur Shelby, a Kentucky farmer and slaveowner, is forced by debt to sell two slaves—Uncle Tom and Harry, the young son of his wife's servant Eliza—to a trader named Haley. Eliza hears the discussion, warns Tom and his wife, and runs away with her child, followed by Haley, who is prevented from catching her when she crosses the Ohio River and is aided by helpful citizens. Haley meets two slave-catchers who agree to pursue Eliza and Harry. Meanwhile Tom refuses to run away and is taken by Haley toward New Orleans. Before leaving Kentucky, however, Haley buys several more slaves, and one of them (a young mother whose infant Haley sells without her knowledge) commits suicide.

Some time later, Eliza's husband, George Harris, himself an escaped slave in disguise, discovers that Eliza is headed for Canada and sets out to find and join her. Meanwhile, Eliza and her son have been taken in by a Quaker family and are joined by George to prepare for the next stage of their escape.

Tom, on a Mississippi river boat, meets a little white girl named Eva St. Clare, is touched by her beauty and gravity, and rescues her from drowning. Eva's father buys Tom from Haley at Eva's request, and Tom accompanies the family (father, daughter, and cousin Ophelia) to their New Orleans home. There he meets Eva's mother, a spoiled and bigoted woman, and other slaves belonging to the household. He and Eva form a close relationship; by reading to Tom from his Bible, Eva herself grows to understand and love Christianity.

George and Eliza Harris, with their child and two other escaped slaves, are being driven to the next stop on their journey when pursuers overtake them. George wounds one with his pistol; the rest of the posse flees. Eliza persuades the others to bring the wounded man with them to be treated.

Back in New Orleans, Tom has been given the responsibility of marketing for the St. Clare household. St. Clare writes a letter to Tom's wife in Kentucky, informing her of Tom's whereabouts and well-being. St. Clare also buys a young slave girl called Topsy and "gives" her to Ophelia to raise.

Back in Kentucky, Tom's wife, Chloe, convinces Mrs. Shelby that Chloe should be hired out to a confectionary baker in Louisville and her wages saved to buy Tom's freedom. The Shelbys' son, George, writes back to Tom with this news.

After two years, it becomes apparent to Tom—and soon to others—that Eva is terminally ill. Her father refuses to see the truth of this. But after a visit from St. Clare's plantation-owner brother and the brother's young son, Eva's condition worsens, and St. Clare finally must accept the knowledge that she is dying. As death approaches, Eva touches the hearts of all around her, even Topsy, with her sweet Christian acceptance, and when she dies, everyone mourns her. Tom's influence at this point brings St. Clare almost to belief in Christ, and the man promises Tom his freedom, signs Topsy over to Ophelia legally, and begins to make provisions to protect all of his slaves from sale, should something happen to him. But then St. Clare is killed suddenly, and his wife sells most of his servants, including Tom.

Tom's new owner is Simon Legree, a plantation owner, who also buys two women, one intended as the sexual slave of Legree's black overseer Sambo, the other (a 15-year-old named Emmeline) for Legree himself. They are taken to the man's run-down plantation among the swamps. Tom is set to picking cotton, and he tries to make the best of his position by prayer and hope. He meets Cassy, Legree's black concubine, and learns her horrifying story. Tom is whipped mercilessly for attempting to help his fellow slaves, and Legree vows to break his spirit or kill him. Cassy does her best to use her influence to save Tom.

Back in the Midwest, Tom Loker has warned the Quakers that Eliza and her family are being sought at the Lake Erie port where they expect to cross into Canada, so Eliza disguises herself and is not recognized. She, George, and Harry cross into freedom.

But Tom, in the months that follow his beating, loses heart and nearly his faith, until at the lowest ebb of his life he is given the grace to prevail in spirit against Legree's torture. He brings his own spiritual strength to the other slaves, and Cassy devises a way for her and Emmeline to escape. The two women hide in Legree's own garret while the man searches the swamps for them. Legree questions Tom, who knows their plan but refuses to tell. Legree has Sambo and the other overseer whip Tom until he is near death; finally Legree gives up, and the dying Tom forgives him and the two men who whipped him.

George Shelby, arrived to buy Tom's freedom, is in time only to hear his last words. But Cassy and Emmeline have made good their escape, and they meet George on the riverboat going north. Another lady on the boat reveals that she is George Harris's sister, and Cassy recognizes that George's wife Eliza is her own daughter. The two, with Emmeline, go to Canada and find George, Eliza, and their children; they all eventually go to France, return, and plan to emigrate to Liberia. Meanwhile George Shelby returns to his farm, where his father has died, breaks the news to Chloe of Tom's death, and frees all his slaves, telling them to remember that they owe their freedom to the influence of Uncle Tom.

List of Characters

Uncle Tom   The central character, a slave belonging to Shelby.

Eliza and George Harris   Mrs. Shelby's servant and her husband; they have a young son, Harry.

Arthur, Emily, and George Shelby   A Kentucky farmer (Tom and Eliza's owner), his wife, and teenaged son.

Aunt Chloe   Tom's wife; she is the Shelbys' cook.

Dan Haley   A slave trader.

Tom Loker and Marks   Slave-catchers.

Senator and Mrs. Bird   An Ohio couple who help Eliza.

Simeon and Rachel Halliday   A Quaker couple who help Eliza.

Augustine, Marie, and Eva St. Clare   A New Orleans man who buys Tom from Haley; his wife; and their daughter.

Ophelia St. Clare   St. Clare's cousin from Vermont.

Adolph, Mammy, Jane, and Rosa   Some of St. Clare's slaves.

Topsy   A little slave girl whom St. Clare buys for his cousin.

Simon Legree   A plantation owner who buys Tom at auction.

Sambo and Quimbo   Legree's slave overseers.

Cassy   Legree's slave mistress and Eliza's mother.

Character Map

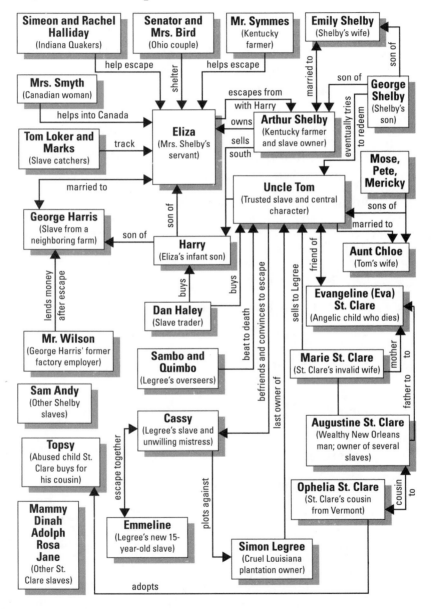

CRITICAL
COMMENTARIES

Chapter I
In Which the Reader Is Introduced to a Man of Humanity

Summary

On a winter afternoon in the early 1850s, two white men, Shelby and Haley, discuss business in Shelby's dining room on a Kentucky farm. Shelby is preparing to sell two slaves to Haley, a slave-trader: Someone named Tom, a capable, honest, Christian, is one. Haley demands another, and when a small boy comes into the room, Haley says he wants the child, too. The boy's mother collects the child, and Haley remarks on her marketability, but Shelby refuses to sell her. But the mother, Eliza, hears the trader offer to buy the child and tells her mistress that she fears little Harry will be sold. Mrs. Shelby, not knowing of Shelby's indebtedness, assures Eliza that Shelby would never do such a thing.

Commentary

Shelby's sale of Tom and little Harry is the action that sets both main plots in motion, the first being Tom's story as he is taken south, sold, and eventually resold; the second (which gets well underway before the novel focuses on Tom) being the story of Eliza's escape with her family to Canada.

Theme

We are also introduced here to two of the book's major themes: the effect of slavery upon morality and the family, and the strength of Christianity as a powerful force by which the individual who lives in Christ's grace may overcome all adversity. Although Tom is present in the chapter only by reputation, we learn that Tom is a Christian man, from which his other strengths and virtues flow. Haley's insistence that no "nigger" can be truly honest and his apparent belief that religion and the appearance of religion are the same thing hint at the tension between Tom's spirituality and the materialism of his owners that will become central to the novel. The second theme is introduced as Shelby prepares to separate Eliza from her child, which the narrator makes plain is not something he chooses to do but something the law regarding slaves as property forces him to do. The most unnatural and immoral act possible is the separation of mother and child, and this is what slavery, which regards human beings as articles of property, not only allows but actually requires. Moreover, Haley suggests another of slavery's immoral functions when he tells Shelby that Eliza would sell well in New Orleans; he would sell her into sexual slavery. He does not state this intent for little Harry, but we will learn that both Mrs. Shelby and Eliza are well aware of this possibility for young boys as well as girls.

Style & Language

The point of view in the novel is that of the *omniscient* ("all-seeing") third-person narrator. This narrator (who is, for all intents and purposes, Stowe herself) describes and relates settings, characters, and action; she can also relate the thoughts and feelings of any of the characters (as, for example, she tells us here what Shelby thinks of Haley, but not what Haley himself thinks). Stowe's narrator uses this insight into the minds and hearts of the characters fairly arbitrarily throughout the book, relating some (but not all) characters' thoughts some (but not all) of the time. The narrator may also tell us things about the characters and events, rather than showing them through action (as, for example, she tells us what kind of woman Mrs. Shelby is), and at times she may speak directly to the reader in her own voice, which is sometimes earnest, sometimes angry, sometimes amused, sometimes sarcastic, and so on. Stowe uses this function of the narrator's voice to underscore points made in the book's action.

Literary Device

One of the most important rhetorical strategies throughout the novel is Stowe's use of irony (which may be defined as "a reversal of expectations in service of the truth"). At least four different types of irony operate in Chapter I, and examining each of them will show the reader what to expect in further chapters.

When Shelby, after listening to Haley praise himself, says to Haley, "It's a happy thing to be satisfied," Shelby is using *verbal irony*, saying one thing (and expecting to be understood that way) but meaning another (and enjoying the second meaning privately). The meaning he expects Haley to hear is something like, "I'm glad you admire yourself; you deserve to be admired." The meaning Shelby himself hears (as does the reader) is quite different: "It's lucky you like yourself, because no one with a brain would judge you so well." Characters, as well as the narrator, frequently use this kind of irony; in fact, a character's use of irony is one of the features that Stowe uses to reveal certain characters.

A second form of irony, used by an author to reveal character or for other purposes, is *dramatic irony*. Here, a character's actions or words may seem (to that character, at least) to mean one thing, but the reader (and perhaps other characters) will derive a different meaning. For example, when Haley tells Shelby what a "good-hearted fellow" his former partner, Tom Loker, was, Shelby and the reader know, from what Haley has said about the man, that Loker is cruel and brutal. Thus what Haley expects Shelby to learn (and what he may well believe himself) is different from what we and Shelby *do* learn, which is that Haley himself is insensitive to Loker's real character.

The narrator employs a third form of irony, *sarcasm* (really a type of verbal irony), in the chapter title and again when she comments directly that "humanity comes out in a variety of strange forms now-a-days." In the kind of verbal irony illustrated previously, the speaker hid his true intent from the listener; in sarcasm, however, the speaker's real meaning is apparent in tone of voice. Sarcasm is easy to recognize when heard, but written sarcasm is more difficult to convey; for example, the sarcasm in Chapter I's title is not apparent until we have read the chapter and realize that what Stowe really means is that slavery allows someone like Haley to behave in inhuman ways and still to refer to himself as "a man of humanity."

Character Insight.

But the chapter title may have a second, deeper meaning, and may reveal a fourth (and deeper) form of irony. Shelby, as he is described, really *is* a "man of humanity"—or would be, were it not that slavery forces him and everyone who willingly participates in it to behave as inhumanely (and inhumanly) as Haley himself. Is Shelby a good man and Haley a bad one? This is a question the novel will ask, in various forms, again and again, and Stowe's answer is always that, whatever the intent, an action that promotes or supports slavery (and finally even inaction, the failure to take action against slavery) is bad. The irony here is *situational irony* and is implicit in the whole situation, the whole fact of slavery. We *expect* an obvious gentleman like Shelby to behave in moral and admirable ways, while an obvious boor like Haley will display behavior immoral and reprehensible. Ironically, however, Shelby himself is as bad as Haley or worse, for he has the advantages of education and cultivation that should allow him to make better decisions.

Throughout the book, Stowe will employ these forms of irony alone and in combination. The narrator's voice, especially, is ironic and usually understated—as when, in a later chapter, she tells of a slave weeping because he has been sold without having a chance even to tell his wife:

"Poor John!—the tears that fell, as he spoke, came as naturally as if he had been a white man." This sentence must be heard in the narrator's characteristic tone of deadpan sarcasm if it is not to be read as the remark of an imbecile.

Glossary

quadroon   a person of mixed race whose ancestry includes one grand-parent of African descent and three of European. (*Quadroon, octoroon*, and similar terms were used to make distinctions in a complex system of social and legal status developed in some Caribbean societies. In the United States, they were apparently used less exactly; Stowe uses *mulatto* throughout the novel to refer to people of mixed race, and *quadroon* to refer to African-American people very light in complexion, even when the person's exact ancestry is not known.)

Jim Crow   a generic name formerly used by Southern whites for African and African-American people, especially boys or young men; used slightingly.

Wilberforce   William Wilberforce (1759–1833), English statesman and vigorous opponent of slavery.

Chapters II and III
The Mother; The Husband and Father

Summary

In Chapter II, the narrator pauses to describe Eliza as a young woman of beauty and grace, gently raised from childhood by Mrs. Shelby, and to tell of her marriage to George, who is the slave of a Shelby neighbor named Harris. Earlier in their marriage, Eliza lost two children in infancy, which makes her especially protective of little Harry. When Eliza and George were married, George was "hired out" to the owner of a small factory, where he was a superior employee and invented a labor-saving machine. His jealous owner ended George's factory employment, assigned him to menial labor, and now punishes him gratuitously. George can keep from expressing his anger only by exercising strict self-control.

In Chapter III, later in the afternoon, after Mrs. Shelby has left, Eliza's husband George, on an errand for his master, stops to see Eliza and their child. George complains bitterly about his life and tells Eliza that his master has decided to make him take a different woman as his wife. George says he plans to run away to Canada, where he will work and try to buy Eliza's and Harry's freedom.

Commentary

These two chapters finish laying the groundwork for the Eliza plot, and they introduce the character George Harris. Eliza and George are two important characters in the book, as they are the central characters of the second plot. Neither, however, is really a developing character. Eliza is a stereotypical young mother of sentimental fiction, conventionally beautiful, conventionally attached to husband and child. It is the loss of her first two babies that makes her attachment to Harry strong enough to support her behavior in later chapters, which the narrator does not fail to remind us, for that behavior is *not* that of a conventional sentimental heroine. We are also told, later, that Eliza's character has matured and deepened, but in fact this is never actually shown, for as a *character* Eliza is less important than she is as a *type:* Readers who have found this type of character attractive in other books, and who are thus able to identify with Eliza on a conventional level, may be surprised when they realize they are sympathizing and identifying with a woman of color; this of course may have been Stowe's purpose in so portraying Eliza.

Character Insight

George, too, is a conventional sentimental hero with enough spirit and spark in him to make him probably more attractive to a modern reader than is his wife. We like George almost immediately for his anger, for his outraged assertion that he is a better man in every way than his master. We like him for his adventurous spirit, his willingness to undergo hardships and take risks. Conventionally, all this is for his wife and child, but as George is portrayed, we suspect that he would be as bold and adventurous even if he were not married. Much later in the novel, we learn that George is studious and philosophical, but we see him throughout as a man of action, and he does not really change. Like Eliza, George is a relatively *static* character, functioning as a type rather than as an individual. Although he plays a relatively small part in the book, he is the most thoroughly likeable, albeit the most conventional, of its male protagonists. Again, this may have been Stowe's intent: Male and female readers would both have found George attractive, and white readers would not have seen him as exotic or alien. Even George's assertive masculinity cannot make him seem threatening, for he is domesticated by his loving marriage and is a faithful husband to the beautiful Eliza, another characteristic of his type as found in the fashionable fiction of the day.

It is worth mentioning that George and Eliza are both said to be very light-skinned. This fact is significant in several ways. First, of course, the possibility of their "passing" as white or Latino people will be necessary to the plot in later chapters. Second (and the novel will recognize this but will not explore it in any depth) the fact that both of these characters, and several others of mixed race) are virtually "white" is ironic, given the argument that was advanced by proponents of slavery that Africans and people of African descent were somehow intended by God and / or by nature to be enslaved. However foolish and self-serving this argument may seem to us, it is one of the many proslavery arguments that Stowe must deal with in the novel, and one way of doing so is to show that many slaves could not be readily identified as to race. A third significance of George and Eliza's being light-skinned is one that we may consider racist: Since Stowe's intended audience was white, it may be that she believed readers would be more likely to sympathize or identify with people who resembled themselves, and thus that white readers would find it easier to see the beauty of the mixed-race Eliza than they might have found it to see the beauty of a dark-skinned African woman.

We may see yet a fourth kind of significance in this aspect of the characters George and Eliza. Eliza fears the loss of her little son, knowing that slavery can separate children from their mothers. But she herself was raised since she was a child by Mrs. Shelby. Her own mother must have been a slave from whom Eliza herself was separated in childhood. Furthermore, Eliza fears the immoral use that her child may be put to, should Haley resell him, and the narrator tells us that Mrs. Shelby has protected Eliza herself from the all-too-common fate of attractive young girls and women in slavery. Yet Eliza's own mother, whoever she was, must have suffered that fate herself, if a white man fathered the light-skinned Eliza. In fact, George and Eliza, like the other mixed-race characters in the novel, testify by their skin color to the immorality of a system that separates families, will not allow slaves to marry legally, and holds individual men and especially women hostage to the sexual and commercial wants of those who have power over them.

Glossary

bagging   cloth for making bags; George's factory apparently manufactured cloth made from hemp.

Whitney   Eli Whitney (1765–1825), American inventor of the cotton gin, a machine for separating cotton fibers from the seeds.

Chapter IV
An Evening in Uncle Tom's Cabin

Summary

The narrative is interrupted again for a description of Uncle Tom and his family. His "cabin" is described as a one-room log house. Inside is Tom's wife, Aunt Chloe, preparing an evening meal. Two young boys, Mose and Pete, are playing with a baby girl about a year old; these are Tom and Chloe's three children. The family has a guest, the Shelbys' son George, who is teaching Tom to write and is going to stay for supper. While the meeting is taking place, the scene changes briefly to the Shelby dining room, where Shelby is settling his debt to Haley. Haley promises, unconvincingly, to try to find a good home for Tom.

Commentary

Literary
Device

This chapter is in the form of a literary *sketch*, a short, mostly descriptive narrative, popular in Stowe's time and a form in which she often worked. The ironies implicit in the chapter may not be immediately apparent, for reasons related to differences in audience. In Chapter IV, we have a picture that would have seemed on the surface (in 1852) to show the slave, Tom, as a respected man with a comfortable and picturesque home, well-treated by his master's family, secure among his own wife, children, and friends, leading them all in heartfelt Christian worship. Those early readers who wanted to believe slavery was a good or at least an acceptable thing would have been able to relax and smile at this chapter. Such readers, however, were being set up: Stowe is again employing situational irony, for the narrator and the reader both know what has transpired in the first chapter. They know this happy home is about to be destroyed, and she makes that irony explicit in the short final scene of the chapter.

Unfortunately for the author's rhetorical plan, readers today are not likely to be lulled into relaxation by this depiction of happiness in the slave quarters. To be sure, not every 1852 reader would have been smiling either; no doubt many of them cringed as we do at Chloe's jovial flattery of young "Mas'r George" and at that young man's tossing of food at his contemporaries, the sons of his host and hostess, as those two "woolly-headed" youths roll happily on the floor. But the very ugliness of the stereotypes may keep us from seeing what is really going on in the chapter.

First, the description of the cabin makes the place seem comfortable and homey, but a comparison with "the halls of the master" is always implied and finally stated. We see a family of five living in one room made marginally comfortable only by the labor and effort of people who spend most of their day seeing to it that the master and his family are much more comfortable. Aunt Chloe's bread and cake and molasses, her rickety table and cracked teapot, are made to contrast with the fine foods she prepares and serves in the master's well-appointed house. For readers who look at the details of this sketch, the contrasts undercut the sentimental prettiness of chinked logs and climbing roses.

The offensive stereotypes (Aunt Chloe flattering and fooling with the white boy, while she snaps at her own sons and calls them "niggers," Uncle Tom humbly taking a lesson in the alphabet from his owner's child) are similarly undercut for readers who look more closely. For the reader who defended slavery as a kindly, paternalistic institution, George's presence is more evidence of the good will between slaves and their owners. In fact, however, this glimpse into Tom and Chloe's cabin and life is a carefully drawn picture of what any white visitor or owner might have seen, designed to let us see these people as they pretend to be while their masters are watching: carefree, happy, joking, singing, the "childish darkies" so dear to the hearts of slavery's defenders.

Character Insight

"Uncle" Tom, the novel's central character, is seen here for the first time. From this chapter we know that he is quietly studious, helpful, earnestly prayerful, kind, fond of children, and almost preternaturally patient and forbearing. As the book progresses, Tom's character will not so much *develop* as it will be *revealed*; he will be put into situations and tested, for central to his character is his steady, unshakable Christian faith. It is worth noting that, whatever stereotypes the name "Uncle Tom" may now suggest, Tom as he appears in the novel is no stereotype. He is described as a "powerfully-made" man, dark-skinned, with "truly African" features and an air "self-respecting and dignified, yet united with a confiding and humble simplicity." His age is not suggested, but he and his wife are young enough to be the parents of a baby and two sons not yet in their teens; we are later told that Tom is about eight years older than Shelby, his owner (who may be deduced to be between 35 and 40 when the novel opens), so Tom is probably somewhere in his middle 40s, not the white-haired old man of later illustrations and dramatizations.

"Aunt" Chloe, on the other hand, does behave in this chapter like the stereotype of the foolish, fawning slave woman that 1960's black radicals called "Aunt Jemima." She jokes, flatters, pretends to be inordinately proud of herself, pretends to side with "her" white family against her fellow slave, Jinny, a neighbor's cook. Her treatment of her sons is in marked contrast to her treatment of George Shelby, and they obviously don't resent this; in fact, they seem to follow her clowning example. Here is a game their mother plays, one that they are learning. A moment of real camaraderie among the three boys is heartrending, because we know this possible friendship will only become another master-slave relationship, full of false pleasantry at best. Later, we will see Chloe as she is without pretense, and the contrast will become another irony: Aunt Chloe is not what she seems.

Glossary

rusk   sweet, raised bread or cake, sliced and toasted or baked a second time.

Mericky   Chloe calls the baby girl "Mericky," perhaps short for "America"; in a later chapter, she will call the child "Polly."

trundle-bed   a low bed on small wheels or casters, that can be rolled under another bed when not in use.

parchment   a document written or printed on parchment.

Chapters V–VII
Showing the Feelings of Living Property on Changing Owners; Discovery; The Mother's Struggle

Summary

Later that evening, Mr. Shelby tells his wife that he has sold Tom and little Harry. Mrs. Shelby is horrified; he has promised Tom his freedom, and she has assured Eliza her child is safe. Shelby admits that Haley held a mortgage on their property and that he was forced to choose between selling those two and selling everything, including all their slaves. Mrs. Shelby says she always knew slavery was evil; now she dreads having to tell Eliza.

But Eliza has overheard. She packs what she can and leaves the house, carrying her child and few possessions. She goes first to warn Tom and Chloe, and Chloe urges her husband to run away, too, but Tom refuses, saying Eliza is right to go but he has no choice except to fulfill his master's bargain. Tom looks at his sleeping children and weeps. Eliza asks them to tell her husband what she has done and that she will try to make it to Canada.

The next morning, Eliza is found missing. Haley arrives and the other slaves lose no time in telling him Eliza and the boy are gone; Haley is persuaded, with some difficulty, that Shelby was not an accomplice in their leaving and that he will assist in a search for them. Shelby delegates two slaves, Sam and Andy, to join Haley in searching. Sam, perceiving that Mrs. Shelby is not eager that they find the fugitives, manages to delay the search.

In Chapter VII, Eliza dreads leaving her home but prays for the strength to succeed. She carries the child all night along the main road toward the Ohio River. At daylight she hopes they will be taken for white travelers and will be safe unless someone recognizes them. She buys a meal at a farmhouse, where the white woman is not suspicious. Near sunset Eliza rents a room to wait for a boatman who will take them across the Ohio, for the river is jammed with ice and the ferry will not run.

Meanwhile Chloe and other servants delay Haley's search even longer, and Chloe comments upon the trader's chances for salvation (which she sees as slim). Several children agree, but Tom tells them they ought to pray for the man. Shelby calls for Tom and informs him that he has been sold; Tom reduces his former master to tears with the reminder that they have been together since Shelby was an infant. Mrs. Shelby tries to get Haley to promise that he will resell Tom to her husband in a year.

The search begins, on horseback. Sam maneuvers Haley into taking the wrong road, and they lose several more hours. When they finally reach the village where Eliza is staying, it is almost dusk. Sam spots Eliza at a window and makes a diversion that gives her time to wake Harry and run out the inn door toward the river. Haley sees her and gives chase, but Eliza jumps onto a huge floating chunk of ice. Carrying the boy, she leaps from cake to cake of ice as her pursuers watch in horror and amazement. She reaches the Ohio side and is helped onto shore by a Kentucky farmer who recognizes her but has no desire to return her to Shelby. He directs her to a house where she can get help. Seeing all this, Sam and Andy leave Haley and head for home.

Commentary

Thus Eliza's northward adventures get underway before Tom's journey southward has begun, and the novel's two plot lines separate, a separation that will make for reader interest as we are taken from one setting, group of characters, and often suspenseful action to another, a strategy that must have been especially good for magazine sales when the story first appeared in serial form.

The Eliza plot involves numerous characters, mostly minor, who help Eliza and her family to escape. The first of these are Sam, a wily Shelby farmhand, aided by the servant Andy; Chloe and her helpers in the kitchen; and Mrs. Shelby herself, who sees what these characters are doing and does not openly encourage them but does her best to assist in slowing down the search. Eliza's first helper on the northern side of the Ohio is a sympathetic Kentuckian who admires her courage. We should remember that, although escaped slaves who had crossed into a "free" state could have been captured and returned to the south in previous years, only after the passage of the Fugitive Slave Act (which took effect in 1851) were citizens of the free states forbidden by law to help these fugitives, a development that not only led many Northerners to break the law but also forced escapees to travel farther, all the way to Canada, if they wanted to be sure of their freedom.

The portrayal of characters in these chapters bears some examination. Chloe, in her bitter reaction to Eliza's news, demonstrates that her clowning in Chapter IV was only an act. She is prepared to flatter her owners, to play the game as expected and teach it to her children, but she is not able nor does she try to hide her anger and grief at Tom's sale. Moreover, the exchange between Chloe and Tom in the kitchen, as she prepares to serve lunch, illustrates the specific character of Tom's Christian fortitude. Chloe meets Tom's suggestion (that they ought to pray for the trader rather than curse him) with the retort that praying for Haley does not seem to be in her nature. It is *not* natural, Tom tells her; but we are required by Christianity to overcome nature, which we can do with Christ's grace. Tom's statement here, one of the first we hear him make, clearly expresses not only his strongest character trait but also one of the book's chief themes.

The Shelbys appear here as flat characters, existing to further the plot, not very interesting except as they contrast with the two other married couples we have met so far. For the sake of plot and theme, we must take at face value Shelby's claim that he really had no choice but to sell Tom and Harry, and although we do not know how much money was involved, we may deduce from sums mentioned later in the book (and Haley's claim, likely understated, that Eliza would bring "over a thousand" on the New Orleans market) that Shelby really has nothing else of so much value that he might have sold instead. Yet the man's apparent regret at this necessity, expressed in snappishness at his wife's shocked reaction, shows up rather badly against Tom's wholehearted grief. For that matter, Mrs. Shelby's embarrassment and even her bold pronouncement on the evils of slavery lose some force when contrasted with Eliza and George's willingness to risk all personal safety and well-being in order to preserve their family. We cannot help but consider other ways in which Mrs. Shelby might have reacted; she might, for example, have assisted Eliza in her escape, or at least told her at once. Instead, she goes to sleep and wakes to wonder why Eliza is not there to help her dress. Stowe's narrator does not underline the point for us (as she does so many others throughout the book), but it would be hard to miss the fact that it is not the slaves who seem to be made callous and unfeeling by the habit of slavery, but rather the owners who are so affected.

Another character deserving of comment is "Black Sam," the farmhand who sabotages Haley's pursuit of Eliza. Sam is a very minor character, but his performance in these chapters is enough to render him memorable. Because Eliza's escape is almost entirely due to Sam, and because it seems to have been successful, the reader is inclined to applaud his methods, underhanded as they are. Yet a modern reader is likely to be incensed or at least made very uncomfortable by what seems to be (and indeed is) the stereotypical sketch of a "comic" black figure, drawn by a white writer for the amusement of a white audience. Sam mugs and grins, uses big words and gets them wrong, screeches in broad dialect, and seems ready at any moment to break into a comic dance. He is quite willing to capture Eliza, if this will help him to step into the position of trust and responsibility formerly held by Tom, for his eye is to the main chance. We can hardly help laughing at Sam's actions (and at his understudy, Andy, who follows him assiduously), but we hate ourselves for doing so.

Character Insight

However, as with her sketch of the scene in Tom and Chloe's cabin, Stowe is playing to a double audience here. Still early in the novel, the apologists for slavery could smile as they recognized their favorite clichés illustrated in the entertaining character of the comic "darkie." They were being set up for the knockdown punch, the sudden irony at the end of the seventh chapter, where Eliza gets away and Sam and his sidekick leave Haley speechless on the shore of the Ohio. Moreover, a closer reading of the chapters reveals that Sam has turned all the laughter toward Haley, who is made a fool of and who knows he is made a fool of, but can do nothing about it. Far from being slow-witted, Sam picks up instantly on Mrs. Shelby's lack of enthusiasm about the search for Eliza, and he is all too happy to oblige her. Without batting an eye, he assesses the temper of Haley's horse and takes appropriate action immediately, as he does later with the man himself. Unlike Tom, who is bound by moral principle and spiritual commitment to love his enemies and do good to those who persecute him, Sam sees no reason to help those whom Andy calls "the soul-drivers." All of Sam's shuffling and grinning are cover for what he does best, which is to size up the situation and take advantage of it. The last laugh is on those readers who see Sam first and last as an amusing *type*. And it is very nearly the last laugh that they or we will have in this book, which begins now to darken.

Glossary

St. James   palace in Westminster, London: the royal residence from 1697 to 1837.

Coeur de Lion   Richard I (1157–99), king of England (1189–99), called "Richard Coeur de Lion," or Richard the Lion-Hearted.

palm-leaf   a hat woven of palm-leaves or similar material.

"Pray for them that 'spitefully use you"   Matthew V, 44: "Love your enemies, bless them that curse you, do good to them that hate you, and pray for them which despitefully use you, and persecute you" (Christ's words, from the Sermon on the Mount).

"far dogs"   Sam's dialectal version of "fair" dogs, meaning not great dogs, but pretty good ones. Stowe's rendering of various dialects has been praised but is sometimes difficult to interpret.

pike   a highway or main road.

"constitutional relations"   that is, obligations to the law.

Chapters VIII and IX
Eliza's Escape; In Which It Appears That a Senator Is but a Man

Summary

Haley, frustrated by Eliza's escape, goes back to the inn, where he chances to meet his old partner, Tom Loker, accompanied by a man named Marks. Over drinks, Loker and Marks commiserate with Haley and agree that slave women's attachment to their children can be inconvenient. Haley and Loker, getting drunk, begin to argue, and Marks urges them to get back to business. He and Loker are slave-catchers; they propose to catch Eliza and Harry, give the boy to Haley, and take Eliza to New Orleans to sell (they can bribe an official to certify that Marks is her legal owner). Haley gives them $50, to be repaid if they profit as they hope from Eliza.

Meanwhile, Sam and Andy return to the Shelbys and report Eliza's escape, at which both Mr. and Mrs. Shelby are gratified. Sam and Andy then go to the kitchen, where Chloe feeds them and Sam retells the story.

In Chapter IX, the scene is the Ohio home of a state senator, Bird, and his family. The senator has come home from Columbus for a night, and his wife asks him about a law making it illegal to shelter or help a runaway slave. He admits that he voted for the law, but she tells him she will break it at her first opportunity. Their servant calls Mrs. Bird into the kitchen where he and his wife are tending to Eliza and little Harry. The senator watches while his wife and the servants make the fugitives comfortable; he then suggests some articles of clothing that they might give to Eliza. Eliza tells her story, which reduces everyone present to tears. In private, the senator tells his wife that he must take Eliza and the child to the house of a man named John Van Trompe, in a secluded woods some miles from town, where she will be safe from the searchers who are sure to come after her. They start at midnight and arrive at Van Trompe's house after a rough, muddy drive. The man says he can handle Eliza's pursuers if they appear. Senator Bird leaves to catch the stage for Columbus.

Commentary

The pair of slave-catchers, Loker and Marks, together with Haley, form the basis of one of Stowe's interesting sketches, this one not so much humorous as colorful, showing three more or less low-life characters in action around a punchbowl. This scene was quite a challenge to a lady writer in the Victorian 1850s, and yet the sketch holds up well. Loker is the ex-partner whom Haley has mentioned to Shelby as a "good-hearted fellow"; here he is described as a typical "western" character: crude, brutal, blustering, and not very bright. His new partner, Marks, is feline and rather dainty, and the trio is completed by Haley, who is generally good-natured, slick, acquisitive, and who here reveals a tendency to worry while in his cups about his chances of salvation.

Their conversation is ironic: They are shaking their heads sadly, unable to comprehend why "gals" get so all-fired attached to their young ones; it must be a female thing. Yet we recall Haley assuring Shelby that Eliza, like others of her race and sex, will soon get over the loss of little Harry if she is given a new dress or something else to distract her. The effect of the scene is amusing, but chilling when it ends with the exchange of Eliza's shawl and we realize that these three terrible rascals may soon have her in their clutches. Stowe's first readers, many of whom might never have set foot in the barroom of a New England tavern, let alone a Kentucky one, must have been somewhat shocked and faintly titillated; the narrator apologizes, with some more of her deadpan sarcasm: Her readers had better get used to such company, she says, for these are men whose profession is becoming respected.

Literary Device

The irony continues in the next chapter, with Senator Bird proving himself a man of humanity despite his calling as a politician. The conversation between the senator and his wife, just before Eliza's appearance in their kitchen, is the first of several that will be reported, between various characters in the book, upon the subject of slavery. Senator Bird has voted for a fugitive slave law, and he argues that private feelings are all very well but that there are greater interests involved: specifically, in this instance, the interests of the state of Kentucky, which has apparently exercised political pressure upon its neighbor state because of the activity of antislavery proponents in Ohio. Mrs. Bird argues that she doesn't understand politics, but that her Bible tells her to do what she can for those in need, and she intends to do just that, law or no law. The senator hems and haws, but what he has helped to legislate in theory turns out to be something he cannot carry out in practice, and he immediately and without question breaks the law he has just helped to enact.

The Birds are flattish characters, as befits their very brief appearance in the novel, and yet one feels Stowe's affection for them as one feels her faint dislike of the Shelbys. Their home and the surrounding country must have been a pleasure for Stowe to describe, especially the "corduroy road" over which Cudjoe and the senator drive with Eliza and Harry, as she had recently left southern Ohio at the time of this writing and could draw the detailed description from memory. The fictional incident itself was taken from a real one, in which Stowe's husband and brother supposedly took a young woman to a stop on the "underground railroad" late one night, fording a swollen creek. This detail Stowe left out of Chapter IX, perhaps thinking that such another harrowing adventure, so soon after Eliza's crossing of the icy river, would be too much to be believed.

Glossary

olla podrida   (Spanish) a stew; or, by extension, any assortment or medley.

peach-blow   peach blossom.

bombazin   bombazine; a heavy, twilled silk cloth, often dyed black.

railroad   a road made from rails; here, a "corduroy" road, a road made of logs laid crosswise.

Chapter X

The Property Is Carried Off

Summary

The scene shifts to Uncle Tom's cabin, where Tom and Chloe are about to be parted. The children are enjoying the festive meal (Tom's last breakfast at home) until their parents' unhappiness demonstrates that this is an unhappy occasion. Mrs. Shelby appears to tell Tom goodbye and assure him that she will try to buy him back, but she breaks into tears before she can speak, and Chloe joins her, as do the children. Haley comes in and takes Tom to his wagon, shackling his ankles. Shelby is not there, nor is young George; the boy, visiting at a friend's house, doesn't know that Tom has been sold. At a blacksmith shop, where Haley has stopped to have a set of handcuffs enlarged, George Shelby rides up and assures Tom that, if he were a man, this would not have happened. Tom and George make their farewells, and George gives Tom a silver dollar on a cord to wear around his neck, apparently George's cherished possession. George and Haley exchange unfriendly words, and the trader drives off with Tom.

Commentary

Character Insight

With Eliza on her way northward, pursued by Loker and Marks, the novel's main plot gets underway in earnest, as its central character, Tom, is carried southward. His legs are shackled, for Haley has already lost money on one runaway slave, and he disbelieves Tom's assurances that he won't try to escape. Tom's passivity, as he allows himself to be led and shackled (he has no choice; he has made his choice by refusing to run away when Eliza left), is a function of his religion. Tom is a Christian, and to be a Christian is to follow Christ, to attempt to be Christ-like. Modern readers, especially, prefer Eliza's brand of Christianity and Mrs. Bird's, which calls for active resistance to immoral authority. Tom, who never hesitates to advise others on the morality of their actions, approved Eliza's escape and will later suggest that other characters attempt to escape. But his own strength is in passive non-resistance. Tom is a Christ-figure, and readers (probably

Stowe's original audience as well as ourselves) are made uncomfortable by the self-sacrifice implied in his behavior.

Theme

The theme of Christianity, of the necessity of following Christ no matter how difficult the path (and it will lead Tom very deep into the darkness) is united here as it will be throughout the book with the theme of the great wrong of slavery. Chloe, who is not a believer in passive resistance, would kill Haley if that would do any good; only her realization that she can do nothing keeps her from trying. She rails against Shelby, who has sold Tom, as she puts it, to get out of a scrape, and although Tom chides her for talking against Shelby, she knows there's something wrong somewhere. Of course it is slavery itself that is wrong. Chloe can't put her finger on it, because she is no philosopher and has never known any life but slavery. Nothing so terrible has happened to her; she has minded her own business; she has taken pride in her skill and loved her family and been a good Christian, and now, suddenly, what she never expected to happen has happened. In her own way, Chloe has discovered what will be reiterated again and again in this book: There is no reconciling Christianity and slavery, despite the churches' attempts to do so. This point is made again in a different way when young George Shelby lashes out verbally at Haley, telling him he ought to be ashamed to make his living the way he does. Haley answers that as long as people like George's parents want to buy men and women, the man who sells them is no worse than they are. George has no answer to this; Stowe's point, of course, is that Haley is absolutely correct.

Glossary

"That undiscovered country . . . " Shakespeare, from *Hamlet*, Act III, Scene 1: "The undiscover'd country from whose bourn / No traveler returns . . . "; Hamlet's line refers to death as "the undiscovered country."

limb i.e., "limb of Satan," a phrase meaning "imp" or "devil" (metaphorically, an arm or leg of Satan, doing the devil's work), commonly used as a euphemism.

Chapters XI–XIV
In Which Property Gets into an Improper State of Mind; Select Incident of Lawful Trade; The Quaker Settlement; Evangeline

Summary

In a small-town Kentucky hotel, a stranger inspects a poster advertising a reward for a runaway slave named George, dead or alive. One of the Kentuckians says that if slaves are treated well they won't run away, so he has no sympathy for the man offering this reward. The stranger, who turns out to be the factory owner for whom Eliza's husband once worked, agrees and says he knows this fugitive (it is George Harris).

At that point, another stranger (George Harris disguised as a Latino man) enters, accompanied by an apparent slave whom he calls Jim. He examines the poster, rents a room, and then calls Wilson in for some words in private. He tells Wilson his story: George's older sister was beaten by their master, Harris, and sold to a trader to be taken to New Orleans. George has come back to Kentucky with Jim, another escaped slave who is going to try to free his old mother. Wilson lends George some money and wishes him luck; George is armed with pistols and says the slave-catchers will never take him alive.

Chapter XII returns to Tom's plight: During their journey southward, Haley attends an estate sale where he buys three slaves, including a boy named Albert whose mother is devastated because Haley refuses to buy her, too. Another purchase is John, a 30-year-old man who must leave his wife without saying goodbye. Haley takes his slaves aboard an Ohio riverboat, where they are kept in chains with the freight. Above them, a group of white travelers discusses slavery. Haley also brings aboard a young woman and her infant, whom he has bought through an agent. That evening, Haley sells her baby to another passenger. Tom tries to comfort the mother, but she is inconsolable, and that night Tom awakens to see her run past him and jump overboard to her death. Haley regards this as bad luck.

In Chapter XIII, the scene changes to a cheerful country kitchen in Indiana, where Eliza is sitting with an older white woman, Rachel Halliday, a Quaker. Rachel's husband, Simeon, arrives and tells them that George has arrived in the settlement and will be at their house that evening. Eliza faints. She awakens to find herself in bed, drifts back into sleep, and when she wakes again George and little Harry are both with her. The next morning at breakfast, Simeon Halliday tells George that he and Eliza are being pursued and that they will be taken to their next station that night.

In Chapter XIV, a steamboat travels down the Mississippi, loaded with cotton bales. Tom, now unfettered, sits among the bales reading his Bible. He misses his old home and his family but finds comfort in the Scriptures. Also on the boat is a white man named Augustine St. Clare, traveling with an older woman and a little girl of five or six, his daughter Evangeline, called Eva. The girl wanders all over the boat and talks with the slaves. Tom sees her as angelic. She asks Tom where he is going, and when he tells her he will be sold, she says she will ask her father to buy him. Soon afterward, Eva falls into the water, and Tom rescues her. Her father bargains with Haley to buy Tom and soon does so.

Commentary

Chapters XI through XIV take the novel into its central portion, as the Eliza plot nears its climax and the Uncle Tom plot gets well underway, with three important characters (St. Clare, his cousin Ophelia, and his daughter Eva) making their first appearance, although we have not yet been told Ophelia's name or her relationship to the St. Clares. After Eliza and George's reunion, their plot will be put on hold for several chapters, giving us time to become acquainted with the New Orleans family to which Haley has sold Tom. Also in these chapters, we see the first few of the book's embedded stories, small and often fragmentary sub-plots that involve the histories either of major-plot characters or of minor characters who appear in one or both of the main plots.

As is often the case in this novel, the scene in the Kentucky barroom serves several purposes at once. It begins with another colorful sketch, this one involving several western characters: the Kentucky frontiersman remained, in the 1850s, a figure of some interest to readers in the East and abroad, and here Stowe makes the most of her familiarity with the West and its exotic inhabitants. These westerners, besides looking and acting colorful, argue about the treatment of slaves, which must certainly have been a realistic touch and which gives Stowe the opportunity to state at least two variants of the arguments concerning slavery that her book addresses. The scene presents a broad irony, when the young man wanted dead or alive walks in, looks at his own poster, and is not recognized as an escaped slave; indeed he is taken for a higher class of citizen, because apparently richer than most of the other men in the room. Another argument allows George to state persuasive reasons why he is *not* obligated, as Wilson begins by saying he is, to return to his lawful master: The laws by which he belongs to Harris are not George's laws, nor is the country his country, since it does not extend to him the rights of a citizen. Finally, in Chapter XI, we learn something about George's background and are given the first of the embedded plots, concerning George's sister Emily who resisted Harris's sexual overtures and was thus sold, apparently into sexual slavery, in New Orleans.

The next embedded plots concern slaves whom Haley buys in Kentucky and on his way south. Young Albert and his mother, Hagar, are both offered in an estate sale. The boy is young, strong, intelligent, and his mother is frightened that he will be sold away from her. Pitifully, she tells people that she still has lots of work left in her, although she obviously does not. Albert is her last child, and her master had promised that he would not sell this one as he has all the rest. But the son is a good investment, the mother a poor one, so Haley rejects her plea that he buy her too. Another man bids on her, seemingly out of kindness, and other slaves gather around and try to console her, but of course she will never be consoled. There is another fragmentary plot concerning "John, aged thirty," and still another concerning the young woman whose ten-month-old child is sold by stealth while she looks over the crowd of slaves at the Louisville docks, trying to get a last glimpse of her husband. The effect of these ultra-short stories, here and throughout the book, is to amplify the reader's horror at the emotional carnage wrought by slavery, which substitutes economic motive in the buyers and sellers for every human consideration. Each embedded plot is tiny and more or less incidental to the main plot in which it appears, but as they accumulate, the reader feels their impact like that of multiple small cuts, growing more sensitive to them rather than less.

Although relatively little use is made of symbolism in the novel (and what there is stands out clearly—for example, Tom as a Christ figure, little Evangeline as an angel or "bringer of good news," as her name suggests), ironies are often presented in contrasting images or situations, such as the appearance of George in the Kentucky hotel, apparently a wealthy young man looking at the description of a desperate slave, but really a brave young man looking at a description of himself. Another ironic contrast is found on the riverboat, where the black slaves sit in irons amidst the freight, mourning the loss of their homes and families, while above them white travelers argue whether slavery is ethical.

This scene (and it is a *scene* in the dramatic sense) allows Stowe to connect several of the novel's important themes: the devastation of slavery upon slaves' families, the relative lack of feeling among white people who are not directly involved in slavery, the almost pathological illogic of self-justification among those who *are* directly involved (except for John the drover, who seems to have worked out his feelings about slavery, appearing here as a contrasting figure to the other white Southerners), and the shameful entanglement of the clergy in it all. All of these themes are here on the boat, which slowly and inexorably carries both its passengers and its human freight downstream, south, toward an inevitable climax.

Between the journey down the Ohio and the next phase, down the Mississippi, the book takes us for a refreshing interval to the warm, bustling kitchen of a Quaker farm in the Midwest. If we doubt that the portrayal of the white riverboat passengers is deliberately unflattering, the contrast with the Hallidays and their community convinces us. We find the gentle strength of conviction exhibited by these members of the Society of Friends to be balanced by their plain, direct manner and their refusal to take credit for doing anything but that which is every human being's duty. As humans and as Christians, these characters show up very well against the "Christians" of the riverboat cabin with their dueling scriptural verses.

And finally, on a different boat that takes him more directly southward, surrounded by cotton bales in a foreshadowing of what eventually will befall him, we find Tom visited by the novel's angel of light, little Evangeline St. Clare. The immediate recognition between them is highly ironic, for the contrast between their physical persons and situations could not be greater. Yet Tom and Eva are kindred spirits, and she will now lead him into the series of events that is his fate.

Glossary:

beaver   a man's high silk hat, originally made of beaver fur.

en passant   (French) in passing, by the way.

John Bunyan (1628–88) English writer and preacher who wrote *Pilgrim's Progress*, an allegory of the soul striving for salvation.

Hagar a woman in the Old Testament, concubine of Abraham and slave of Abraham's wife Sarah; the mother of Ishmael. Hagar's slavery and other specific mentions of slavery in the Bible were sometimes cited as evidence that God approved of the institution.

"Rachel weeping for her children . . . " *Matthew* II, 18: refers to Herod's killing the boy children as the fulfillment of this prophecy.

"Cursed be Canaan . . . ." *Genesis* IX, 25: "[H]e [Noah] said: 'Cursed be Canaan; meanest of slaves shall he be to his brethren'"; Noah is cursing his son Ham's child Canaan because Ham looked at his father lying naked and drunk in his tent. One of the justifications cited for slavery was that "Hamites" (supposedly the black African race, a mistaken identification) shared in their ancestor's curse.

brochetelle brocatelle; a heavy, figured cloth like brocade, usually of silk and linen, often used for upholstery.

cestus in ancient times, a woman's belt or waist-band.

Chateaubriand (Vicomte) Francois Rene de Chateaubriand (1768–1848), French statesman and man of letters; he traveled in North America and wrote about his experiences.

"Let not your heart be troubled . . . ." *John* XIV, 1–2: "Let not your heart be troubled. In my Father's house are many mansions: if it were not so, I would have told you. I go to prepare a place for you."

Cicero (Marcus Tullius) (106–43 B.C.) Roman statesman, orator, and philosopher, writer of a classic text on rhetoric.

morocco a fine, soft leather, made originally in Morocco.

inkhorn a small container, formerly used to hold ink.

Chapters XV and XVI
Of Tom's New Master, and Various Other Matters; Tom's Mistress and Her Opinions

Summary

The narrative is interrupted for the history first of Augustine St. Clare and then of his cousin Ophelia. At the St. Clare home, St. Clare says Tom is to be the coachman. They are greeted by the household slaves, including the butler, Adolph, and "Mammy," who had been Eva's (and her mother's) nursemaid and is now Marie's personal servant. A few days later, St. Clare tells Marie that his cousin Ophelia is to take over the burden of housekeeping, and Marie begins to complain about how tiresome and troublesome the slaves are. Her complaints reveal that she makes unreasonable demands. Marie continues to instruct Ophelia on the ins and outs of the household, what she perceives to be the deceitful and lazy nature of slaves, and the "strangeness" of Eva, who puts servants on an equal level with herself; she says that St. Clare won't let her send the slaves out to a whipping-house. St. Clare returns and remarks ironically that their slaves' laziness is certainly unforgivable, considering the example that he and Marie set for them.

In the courtyard, Eva plays with Tom, which offends Ophelia. St. Clare points out Ophelia's hypocrisy; she wants to free the slaves, send them to Africa, and let missionaries deal with them because she herself is a racist. Ophelia admits there is some truth in this, and St. Clare tells her that slaves have so little good in their lives that he would be wrong to begrudge them the love and friendship of his little daughter, who is a true democrat.

At dinner on Sunday, Marie tells St. Clare about that day's sermon, on the subject of order and distinctions in society (a justification of slavery) as ordained by God. St. Clare says slavery is for the convenience of slaveholders. If slavery were to become bad for the economy, he says, preachers would preach against it. Eva comes in, saying she has been listening to Tom sing hymns. She reads the Bible to him; he sings hymns to her. St. Clare says he has heard Tom praying for *him*, and Ophelia remarks that she hopes her cousin will take Tom's prayer to heart.

Commentary

Chapters XV and XVI slow down the action of the novel for description and background information, including embedded narratives of St. Clare, Ophelia, Marie, and Mammy. Except for St. Clare's story, these are very fragmentary, but all contribute to the novel in various ways. Part of the reason for the slowing of the action in this part of the novel, as critics have noted, was Stowe's unfamiliarity with New Orleans (whose descriptions she got from one of her brothers who lived in that city); at this point, as her main plot moves out of the familiar Ohio Valley, the writer seems to hesitate slightly. But she will pick up speed later.

Theme

Mammy's story, like those of other slave characters, illustrates the theme of slavery's effect upon the family, the separation of wife from husband, mother from children. Of course other kinds of loss and separation must have been just as common, and in fact the embedded narratives of "John, aged thirty" and George Harris and his sister Emily deal with men's separation from wife and sister. However, most of these embedded narratives are emotionally affecting from a woman's point of view, especially that of a mother. Perhaps this was inevitable, since Stowe was a woman and a mother who had recently lost a child at the time of writing the book. But this apparent bias may also be due at least in part to the fashionable sentimentalizing of the mother-child relationship common in the mid-nineteenth century and to the fact that many of Stowe's readers were women. Stowe was accustomed (as her narrator's asides to female readers suggest) to working on women's emotional and moral consciousness in her writing; women's political impact could not be direct, but women could make their convictions felt by exerting pressure on their male relatives, as the earlier Senator Bird episode illustrates.

Character Insight

The three adult members of the St. Clare family are interesting in different ways as they function variously in the novel. Cousin Ophelia is a stereotypical New England spinster who serves as a foil to St. Clare in their several long discussions of slavery in a further chapter. St. Clare himself is a conventional Romantic "hero" whose cynical materialism will be in conflict with Tom's spiritualism. And Marie, the spoiled and fast-fading southern belle, exemplifies many of the wrongs of slavery; she is a woman horribly and completely corrupted by the institution.

So far, Ophelia appears only as a stand-in for the reader, allowing the family and situation to be introduced to us as they are introduced to her. Her description and behavior reveal her as very much a conventional type, the small-town New England spinster, brisk and energetic, a sharp-tongued, slightly grim Calvinist. Inasmuch as the type had its basis in fact, Stowe would have been familiar with more than one woman resembling Ophelia, and we feel her presence as a kind of snappy contrast to the languid Louisianans. But although the author seems to approve of Ophelia's energy (even while gently mocking it), she sees the woman's shortcomings as well and allows us to see them, especially as St. Clare points them out to her. As much as any of this novel's characters, Ophelia will develop as her experience broadens.

Character Insight

Ophelia's cousin St. Clare (called both Augustine and Auguste), important as he is in the book, will not really develop as a character: He will change, eventually, but it will be a change forced upon him from the outside and one that the reader will fortunately not be called upon to believe in for very long. At this point, early in his career in the novel, St. Clare appears also as a conventional type, this one a type from literature: the fashionable "Byronic" version of the Romantic hero. He is cynical, careless, handsome, polite, rich, and impeccably dressed. His cynicism lifts only when he interacts with someone he senses is truly good (a rarity), especially an uncorrupted child. He is attractive not least because we feel a dark brooding quality, laced with potential violence, lurking just below the surface. His history makes plain the reasons for all this: His heart has been broken. He has been forced to forsake the woman he truly loved, although (as we will learn in a later chapter) he carries her miniature portrait and a lock of her hair always next to his heart. And while another woman might have healed this wound, he has had the misfortune to marry Marie. This is the difference between, for example, Eliza's George Harris (as a Romantic type) and St. Clare: George is domesticated, softened, and tamed by his love for Eliza and hers for him, whereas there is no one but Eva to soften and tame St. Clare.

St. Clare is able, because of his cynicism and because of the "outsider" status that his Byronic character brings with it, to voice antislavery arguments although he owns slaves. He can discern, and comment upon, the hypocrisy of "colonizationists" like Ophelia and also the hypocrisy of the so-called Christians who defend slavery, and he serves the novel's thematic purposes in both cases. This is a difficult tightrope for a character to walk if he is to maintain anything like integrity; Stowe has solved the problem by making St. Clare constitutionally lazy, ironically distanced from his own situation, and saddled with Marie, who would certainly never stand for her husband's freeing of his slaves.

Character Insight

Marie, the wife with whom St. Clare is unfortunately saddled, is in some ways the most interesting character in the book, certainly the white female character upon whom the white female author spends her most intense (and mostly vitriolic) energy. A modern reader, especially before meeting Marie, may be inclined to sympathize with her at first, upon learning that St. Clare married this beautiful, rich girl in a fit of rebound after (he thought) being jilted by his real love. But Marie is hopelessly corrupt, so much so that she does not have our sympathy for long. An only child, the narrator tells us, Marie was spoiled first by the fondness of her parents, later by the attentions of suitors (for she was, after all, rich, beautiful, and socially desirable), and always by the attendance of slaves who apparently lived only to serve her. Now, bored and unhappy in her marriage, Marie occupies herself by alternately dressing up fashionably and going to bed with "sick headaches." She is sure that she is very unwell. Her husband ignores her; her daughter finds her puzzling, and she spends her life making her slaves miserable.

Marie's primary function in the novel is to exemplify the spoiled, thoughtless slaveowner, the person who without blinking an eye can treat other people like dirt because they are "black" and she is "white." This racial distinction is all but fictional in the case of Marie and some of her light-skinned servants, but it serves to define them for her (in the racial slavery that defines her and her culture) as bad, lazy, stupid, by definition inferior.

Theme

Marie also serves in the novel to illustrate the slaveowner whom slavery ruins as surely as it injures any slave. She is an absolute narcissist; having learned from infancy to see her servants as objects, she sees *everyone* as an object, even her own child. She is really ill, but her illness is of the spirit. She is full of hate, much of it self-hatred; her constant headaches may be seen as punishment she unconsciously inflicts upon herself (for not having achieved the elusive happiness she grew up thinking was her birthright and for her belittlement and cruel treatment of her servants, which she cannot consciously recognize but which she must acknowledge on some level). Her headaches may also be seen as one of the only forms of feeling possible for Marie, who is incapable of real love or even of real grief, as shall be seen.

Above all, Marie's unhappiness seems to be symptomatic of a sort of sadomasochistic relationship that she carries on with several of her hapless servants, especially Mammy (who also suffers from frequent headaches) and Rosa (who is an attractive and relatively carefree young woman). Significantly, these servants are women; Marie might be seen to have projected herself onto them somehow, or perhaps only to recognize, unconsciously, their potential relationship to her not as objects but as human beings. But to sense that possible relationship must be intensely frightening to someone like Marie, and so the actual relationship, as she shapes it, is this: They make her suffer, and she makes them suffer.

Glossary

Huguenot   any French Protestant of the sixteenth or seventeenth centuries.

hartshorn   ammonium carbonate, used in smelling salts, so called because formerly made from deer antlers.

sick-headache   migraine (or any headache that causes nausea).

Sandwich Islands   former name for the Hawaiian Islands.

colonizationist   one who supported the abolition of slavery with concurrent colonization of Africa by freed American slaves.

arabesque   a complex and elaborate decorative design of intertwined lines suggesting flowers, foliage, animals, etc.

distingue   (French) having an air of distinction; distinguished.

opera-glass   a small binocular telescope.

daguerreotype   a photograph made by an early method on a plate of chemically treated metal.

vinaigrette   a small, ornamental box or bottle with a perforated lid, for holding aromatic vinegar, smelling salts, etc.

Chapter XVII
The Freeman's Defence

Summary

At the Halliday's house, George and Eliza discuss their future in Canada but recognize the dangers they will face before they arrive there. The man who is to drive them to their next stop, Phineas Fletcher, arrives and says their pursuers are gathered in a nearby tavern and plan to chase them down that night. They leave after an evening meal. Near dawn an outrider, Michael Cross, tells them the posse is approaching. Phineas drives to a place where they climb up a steep hillside and take shelter among rocks.

The pursuers—Loker, Marks and others—must come up the trail one at a time. George calls down that he is a free man and will shoot them one by one. The men below tell each other that George doesn't mean it, but only Loker dares go up. George shoots him with a pistol, wounding Loker. Marks, supposing his partner is dead, mounts and rides away. The others also retreat, leaving Loker. As the fugitives begin to walk down the road, they are met by the wagon and men from the next farm. Eliza talks them into loading Loker into the wagon to be cared for at their next stop.

Commentary

Modern readers who have seen more than one action-adventure film or television show set in the Old West can easily envision the setting of this chapter, and while the rocky defile through which these pursuers are challenged to ascend may be the only one of its kind in Indiana, the excitement of the long ride through the night, the breathless chase, the scramble up the rocks, and George's heroic defiance must have quickened the blood of readers who would not have known so well what to expect.

Some aspects of this scene may not be as clear to modern readers, however, as they probably were to Stowe's original audience. The constables who have joined Loker and Marks in their pursuit of these fugitive slaves may or may not have been corrupt, but they were duly constituted officers of the law, acting within their authority, and had thus (no doubt) officially deputized not only the two slave-catchers but also the accompanying adventurers whom Loker and Marks had handily found in the nearby tavern. Riff-raff though this group may appear, it is not *just* a semi-drunken mob, but a semi-drunken mob representing the government, and so George's (and Phineas Fletcher's) defiance of it is a criminal act, an act of civil disobedience. We must remember, therefore, what George told Wilson in an earlier chapter: The government of the United States is not *his* government. He sees himself as a legitimate rebel against a tyrannical authority, and the exchange between George and one of the constables makes clear the terms upon which they meet.

Literary Device

George does not acknowledge the government this lawman represents. To underscore this point, the narrator makes an ironic comparison: If this were a fugitive from some tyranny in Europe, escaping from a repressive and inhuman government, we would consider him a hero; however, since he is a fugitive from our own government, trying to save his wife from sexual slavery and his son from being sold at auction, no reader (she says sarcastically) will applaud him, for we are too patriotic. The efforts of Hungarian patriots against Austrian oppression were, when Stowe was writing, widely admired by the American press and consequently by the public, so her narrator's observation was a timely one.

The cowardliness of Marks and the posse, after George makes his impassioned speech and especially after Loker goes down, is perhaps extremely lucky for the fugitives, but it is not as unbelievable as some readers have complained. The dainty Marks, as the earlier chapter in which he appeared has prepared us to suspect, now shows his true colors. This man whom the narrator has described as cat-like is no fool, and now that his protector Loker appears to be dead, Marks no longer deems the possible reward equal to the risk. Furthermore, Marks and certainly the rest of the group have been telling each other one of the racist stories current at the time: Black men will fight each other but will not fight white men. The pursuers would all like to believe this, but the very fact that they have had to remind themselves of it shows that they aren't actually sure, and George first shakes their faith with his speech and then erases it completely by shooting Loker, so they all turn tail, leaving Loker to die in the road.

Today's reader is likely to bridle at the incident that ends the chapter. The two women in the fugitive party ask that Loker be taken along in the wagon to be treated for his wounds, and the men comply. Earlier, when it seemed Loker might be dead, Phineas, Quaker though he is, hoped it was so; now, of course, even George must agree that the decent thing to do is to pick the man up and get help for him, and we can see the sense in that. But even Jim's old mother, who has been whipped because her son ran away and who now has come within a few inches, literally, of being returned to the same vindictive master, now says she can't help pitying poor Loker, who after all has an old mother himself. It is at this point (especially since we know that Loker is really in no danger of being left) that a reader might be forgiven for a small sin of impatience with such Christian turning of the other cheek; Tom's wife, Chloe, one supposes, would agree.

Glossary

au fait   acquainted with the facts; well-informed.

"But as for me . . . I have put my trust in the Lord God" *Psalms* 73: 2–28.

buffalo   a robe or throw made of buffalo skin.

"Woe unto the world . . ."   See *Luke*, 17: 1, 2: "And he said to his disciples, 'Temptations to sin are sure to come, but woe to him by whom they come! It would be better for him if a millstone were hung round his neck and he were cast into the sea, than that he should cause one of these little ones to sin.'"

own   to acknowledge; George says he does not *own* the laws his pursuers refer to, meaning he does not accept them as his own.

class   people grouped together because of certain likenesses or common traits; in referring to "men of [Loker's] class," the narrator does not mean social or economic class but "men of Loker's type or temperament."

Chapters XVIII–XXI
Miss Ophelia's Experiences and Opinions; Miss Ophelia's Experiences and Opinions, Continued; Topsy; Kentuck

Summary

Back in New Orleans, Tom has duties formerly assigned to Adolph, who has been stealing too much from St. Clare. Tom worries about the state of St. Clare's soul, specifically about his occasional drinking bouts, and finally speaks to his master about this, obtaining St. Clare's promise to mend his ways.

A woman named Prue, who sells hot bread to the St. Clare kitchen, complains about her hard life. Tom hears Prue's story (she was forced to allow her last child to die) and reports it to Eva, who is deeply affected. A few days later, the kitchen staff learns that Prue has been beaten for drunkenness and has died of her injuries. Ophelia, hearing this, asks St. Clare if there is nothing he can do; he tells her that the law will not intervene in such a case. Ophelia asks him how he can defend such a system, and he answers that he does not defend it. For the first time, Ophelia is able to get her cousin to discuss the subject of slavery seriously.

St. Clare's opinion about slavery can be summed up as follows: I have inherited this wrong and can do nothing to right it. People with power always have and always will make unfair use of those without power, and the system of slavery in the southern United States is only one example, albeit an extreme example, of that truth. My efforts to end the system would do no good. Thus, the best I can do is to behave as humanely as possible within the system, treating the slaves I "possess" as well as possible and not blaming them for the faults that the system imposes upon them.

In Chapter XX, St. Clare brings home a small black girl of eight or nine years, whom he presents to Ophelia. His cousin is none too pleased, but St. Clare says the little girl, called Topsy, was being abused by her owners who were using her as help in their tavern. After Ophelia cleans the child up, she finds that Topsy's back is covered with scars and calluses from beatings. She dresses the child and begins to question her, only to find that Topsy knows absolutely nothing about her own history or anything else. She was raised, she says, by a speculator; the servant Jane explains that children are often taken as infants and raised for the market.

In Chapter XXI, the scene shifts back to the Shelby farm in Kentucky. Mrs. Shelby tells her husband that Chloe has heard from Tom, and she asks when he will be able to buy Tom back. Shelby says it is not possible. Chloe, having overheard, tells Mrs. Shelby that she knows of a confectioner in Louisville who would hire her at a good wage, and Mrs. Shelby agrees that Chloe may go.

Commentary

Two embedded narratives appear in Chapters XVIII through XXI, one the story of the unnamed, supposedly incorrigible slave freed by St. Clare, whose life was subsequently saved by the man at the cost of his own life. The first embedded narrative is Prue's story, again featuring a mother from whom every child has been taken. One difference in Prue's case is that the woman had one more child, after being sold away from the master who had taken each of her others, but Prue's new mistress required Prue to leave her sick baby, and the child consequently died. This embedded narrative becomes especially effective when we learn of Prue's death, a horrifying death not only because of the physical circumstances but because Prue has told Tom she would rather go to hell than to heaven, if heaven is where white people go. By Tom's (and Stowe's) lights, as we know from the episode of St. Clare's drunkenness, Prue's chances of salvation are bleak; thus on top of everything else slavery did to this poor woman, it has endangered her soul's salvation.

The first three of these chapters, although Ophelia's experiences take center stage, are more concerned with St. Clare's opinions, as Ophelia insists that he reveal them. The friendly but sharp exchanges between the two cousins become a method by which Stowe can voice many of the different arguments concerning slavery that were current when she wrote. St. Clare's argument was a common one, no doubt, not only among intelligent and thoughtful slaveowners, but even among northerners who disapproved of the system. It rests on two premises: first, that there is a difference of degree, not kind, between American racial slavery and the sort of oppression of the powerless that has always taken place everywhere in the world (nineteenth-century England is given as an example); second, that I know, as an individual, that I myself cannot end this oppressive system, so the best (in fact the only) action I can take is to behave decently within the system.

Theme

The first of these premises, in fact, may or may not be correct; certainly the oppression of the English working class was horrifying in the 1850s, and certainly other slaveries (even other racial slaveries, some of them "more terrible," statistically speaking, than that practiced in the United States) have existed and perhaps will exist in the future. On the other hand (as George Harris might have pointed out), the slavery practiced in the United States, with its related laws, was perhaps the first to be practiced in a society whose constitution and professed beliefs should absolutely have prohibited it. But even if the first premise were true, its relevance is questionable. From an ethical Christian point of view (which was Stowe's point of view), wrong is wrong even if everybody does it. And St. Clare's second premise, of course, is defeated by the same ethical imperative: Right is right, and even if you know you cannot accomplish it, you must try.

Character Insight

St. Clare's voicing of this flawed argument signals a deepening of his character, of the relationship between him and his slaves (especially Tom), and of the tension that will lead to the book's climax. Tom, apart from his singing hymns to Eva, trying to comfort Prue, and communicating with his family in Kentucky, appears hardly at all in these chapters, and yet his first specific action reported in Chapter XVIII is a significant one: After helping Adolph to carry St. Clare into the house one night, Tom speaks to his master about the endangerment St. Clare causes to his soul with such behavior. St. Clare, as we are given to understand, could hardly care less about his soul, and although he might be thought to feel some shame at being falling-down drunk in front of his daughter, the child is fortunately in bed by the time he arrives in this condition, which is apparently not an infrequent occurrence. But he is touched by Tom's concern, promises to reform, and keeps his promise. This development strengthens what we already know of Tom's and St. Clare's characters: Tom, a courageous Christian, is able, humbly but at a real risk to his life, to try to do good for someone who holds absolute power over him. St. Clare is not merely indulgent of his slaves out of laziness tinged with guilt but actually does respect them as human beings, respecting Tom even when he does not share Tom's beliefs.

The incident also has a significance that we might call mythic and that signals a growth in power for Tom that is ironic but also more than ironic. In St. Clare's basically secular culture and time (and to some extent still in our own), many men traditionally delegate matters of morality and religion to their wives (which, in fact, reveals how little importance they actually attach to such matters, despite what they may say or even think they believe). But by delegating moral authority to women, Western (especially "Christian") secular culture has shaped itself in some interesting ways. There has long been a tendency, for example, for people to regard such Christian strengths as Tom exhibits as somehow unmanly, as weaknesses in fact, causing nominal Christians either to reject religion entirely or to ignore the main teachings of its holy book, the New Testament. At the same time, those who practice those teachings (or who act in accordance with other spiritual or mystical beliefs that honor passivity, non-retribution, and non-violence) are able to and often do exercise a powerful influence that may be misunderstood but cannot be denied by the majority culture. This is the sort of power that Tom is beginning to exercise over St. Clare, a power that would, under other circumstances, have been exercised (with less effect) by the women in his life, except that his mother (who once did exercise that power) is dead, his wife has no interest in doing so, and his daughter is still too young. This power, now wielded by Tom, will at last save St. Clare but will not do so in time to save (in the worldly sense) Tom himself.

Another facet of one of the book's important themes, the effects of slavery upon family and morality, is illustrated again in Chapter XX within one of the major plot lines, in the introduction of a new character, young Topsy. As a character, Topsy's basic function in the novel seems to be much the same as her function in the St. Clare household: to force Ophelia's growth from a kind of sounding board for her cousin's cynicism (and an audience for Marie's meanness) into a conflicted and then, finally, a stronger person—in terms of the novel, a stronger character. St. Clare has noted Ophelia's self-contradictory position on slavery: her disapproval of the system, her concern for the education of slaves, especially for their moral education, but also her aversion to his slaves as people.

Ophelia believes that these Africans and African Americans are children of God, and that they are her brothers and sisters in Christ as well, or so she is eager to make them. But she does not want to touch them, and St. Clare has noted her aversion. She shudders when Eva kisses

Mammy or climbs onto Tom's knee, and it seems that Ophelia's aversion may be related to skin color, for Tom is dark-skinned. It is a particularly insidious form of racism, one that seems to have little to do with a belief in the *inferiority* of members of another race, but rather with a physical fear of what is different. Significantly, it seems most often to affect people who have lived entirely apart from members of another race. This is probably to some degree a sexual fear, and it may be significant that Ophelia is an unmarried woman, in middle age, raised in a physically strict home. If this is truly what Ophelia finds troubling, it is a bias not unique to her, or unfortunately to her time. It is, however, a bias that St. Clare does not share.

St. Clare brings Topsy home partly in order to tease his cousin and partly to see what Ophelia will do with the child, who incorporates both facets of Ophelia's self-contradiction: Topsy is absolutely ignorant, and she is very dark-skinned. (Of course, to use a child as a kind of human guinea pig in this fashion might have been seen as unnecessarily cruel even in the 1850s, but Stowe has made it clear that Ophelia is a kind woman, that St. Clare is well aware of her kindness, and that in buying Topsy St. Clare saved her from owners who abused her both physically and mentally.) So Topsy's effect upon Ophelia, although it is not an immediate effect, is eventually to force the middle-aged spinster to confront her own racism.

Character Insight

For the time being, however, Topsy illustrates with horrifying psychological accuracy one of the problems that America's racial slavery created. She is a child who was taken from her own parents in infancy, raised on what amounted to a child-farm, nursed and cared for minimally by other slaves who had so many children to nurse and care for that they had neither the time nor the inclination to teach the children anything. Traditionally, Topsy has been considered a sort of comic character, saying she wasn't born but "just growed"; in fact, Stowe's portrait of the child is tragic. Topsy knows nothing about how old she is or how long she has been with her most recent owners. Topsy is anything but stupid, but her ignorance is abysmal, and both St. Clare and the chambermaid Jane assure Ophelia that there are lots of others just like her, living life as best they can from day to day, waiting for death or for the millennial day, expected or longed for by others, but which they themselves are not even prepared to comprehend, when they will no longer be slaves. But Topsy does know one thing: She is a "nigger," and she has been told this often enough to realize what it means in her society. And she has one set of skills: She is an accomplished thief, a liar, a "wicked" girl who is rather proud of her own wickedness, for it is the only thing at which she has ever been able to excel.

At this point in her life, Topsy is not a sinner; even Ophelia discerns that the child doesn't know she shouldn't lie and steal, doesn't even realize what "wickedness" really is (and therefore isn't really very good at it). But she stands, at eight or nine years old, on the brink of real self-consciousness, and at this point there is nothing to make her choose good over evil. Ophelia, who believes (as almost everyone did in her time) in a judicious use of physical punishment in child-rearing, thinks that perhaps she will have to whip the child; St. Clare remarks that, as Topsy is used to being beaten with a stove-poker, such whippings as Ophelia is prepared to deal out will probably not get Topsy's attention.

This section of the book ends with the receipt of Tom's letter in Kentucky, where Shelby shows his true colors at last, telling his wife irritably that he doesn't know when (or, he implies, if) he can afford to buy Tom back according to his promise. Again, Mrs. Shelby wants to help, but does not extend herself too far to do so. One suspects that modern readers will judge Mrs. Shelby more harshly than Stowe's original audience probably did. Most nineteenth-century Americans, even those who firmly believed that the treatment of human beings as property was a moral outrage, found nothing amiss in the statement that a wife "belonged" to her husband—as of course she still did, in a legal sense, not being able as a married woman to own property or make binding contracts. Still, Mrs. Shelby is here contrasted with Chloe, who plans to work for four dollars a week until she can raise the thousand dollars or so it will take to buy her husband back from St. Clare. (Of course, she will not be buying his *freedom*, for the wages she makes will legally belong, as she herself does, to Shelby.)

Glossary

Joseph in Egypt the biblical Joseph (*Genesis* 37–50), sold as a slave into Egypt, became Pharaoh's trusted servant.

"cost and come to" i.e., outgo and income; budgeting.

meum tuum (Latin) mine and yours; Adolph is said to be confusing what property is his and what is St. Clare's.

"it biteth like a serpent . . . ." *Proverbs* 23:31, 32: "Look not thou upon the wine when it is red, when it giveth his colour in the cup, when it moveth itself aright. At the last it biteth like a serpent, and stingeth like an adder."

Magna Charta   or Magna Carta; literally *great charter*, which King John of England was forced to grant, guaranteeing certain civil and political liberties to his barons, in 1215; here "Magna Charta times" means medieval days, days of lords and serfs.

Muses   in Greek mythology, the goddesses that sponsored the arts and artists; "domestic Muses" would be the (humorously imagined) goddesses who oversee household arts like cooking.

vertu   or *virtu*; artistic objects, such as curios, antiques, etc.

"Sisyphus or the Danaides"   Greek mythological figures; Sisyphus is doomed in Hades to roll a heavy stone uphill, only to have it always roll down again; the Danaides are condemned in Hades to draw water forever with a sieve. Thes allusion is to anyone who must do an endless, pointless task.

the Fates   in Greek and Roman mythology, the three goddesses who control human destiny and life.

"Stay me with flagons . . . ."   *The Song of Solomon*, 2: 5: "Stay me with flagons, comfort me with apples: for I am sick of [with] love."

"When, in the course of human events, . . . "   the opening phrase of the Declaration of Independence; St. Clare is parodying this document.

Solomon   biblical king of Israel: he was noted for his wisdom.

non sequitur   (Latin) a conclusion or inference which does not follow from the premises from which it is drawn; a remark that has no bearing on what has just been said.

dies irae   (Latin) day of wrath; Judgment Day, or, by extension, any solemn day of reckoning.

Chapters XXII–XXV
"The Grass Withereth— The Flower Fadeth"; Henrique; Foreshadowings; The Little Evangelist

Summary

Two years have passed; Tom has learned from the Bible to be content with what he has, and he has become closer to Eva. While the family and servants are at the St. Clare summer house on Lake Pontchartrain, Eva tells Tom she will die soon, and he realizes she is growing pale and thin. Ophelia, too, has noticed Eva's illness, but St. Clare refuses to see or admit it. Marie, however, is oblivious to her daughter's condition.

St. Clare's brother, with his 12-year-old son Henrique, visits at the summer house. Eva and Henrique are going riding. Henrique beats his young groom (another 12-year-old, a slave named Dodo) with his riding whip for a minor offense. Eva calls her cousin wicked and cruel, which surprises him: He has a quick temper, and beating is what one does to slaves. Watching this exchange between their children, St. Clare and his brother get into a discussion about slavery. When the children return, St. Clare is alarmed to see that Eva is feverish and short of breath. Eva tries to make Henrique promise to love Dodo and be kind to him, and, although Henrique finds the idea of loving a slave a strange one, he says he will try to do so for Eva's sake.

Eva now becomes so unwell that her father is forced to call in a doctor. Eva's symptoms abate after a couple of weeks, but although St. Clare takes this for a hopeful sign, the doctor, Ophelia, and Eva herself know that she is dying. Eva tells Tom that she wishes she could give her life for all slaves. She tells her father that she wishes he would free his slaves, for, if anything should happen to him, they would be in bad hands. She makes St. Clare promise that he will free Tom as soon as she dies, and she tries to make him promise to free all his slaves and work for abolition. At last, St. Clare seems to believe that Eva is truly dying.

On a following Sunday, Ophelia finds Topsy cutting up Ophelia's things for doll clothes. She says she doesn't know how to make the child behave; Marie suggests sending her out to be whipped. Topsy admits to St. Clare that she guesses she was just born bad, and Ophelia says she gives up. Eva draws Topsy aside and finds that Topsy has never loved anyone, has never been loved. Eva tells Topsy that *she* loves her, and so does Jesus. St. Clare, watching the children, tells Ophelia she will never get anywhere with Topsy until she can touch her, and Ophelia admits she wishes she were more like Eva, who is Christ-like.

Commentary

Eva's illness, a gradual decline, has had its onset at some point during the two-year period between Chapters XXI and XXII, and now the stage is set for the sequence of events that will move Tom closer to the climax and denouement of his story. Eva's illness, however, is only a signal that a change is coming, for her family and for Tom. Her illness can hardly be said to precipitate the events that come later, but merely to precede them (for, as we shall see, the actual cause-and-effect sequence of events that takes Tom away from New Orleans is something upon which Eva herself could have had no effect). Thus the first function of Eva's illness and slow decline, in terms of the novel's fictional integrity, is to reveal Eva's character, which in a very basic way is unlike that of any of the other three children portrayed in these chapters.

One would probably have to have lived during the nineteenth or perhaps the early twentieth century, in the United States at least, in order to understand the nature of popular response to the illness and death of a child. This subject was widely used in all kinds of literature, from popular songs to children's stories, its pathos exploited for all the tears it could draw forth. The popularity of verse, songs, drama, and fiction based on this subject, at a time when infant and child mortality was still so high that most families lost at least one child to disease or accident, may seem to us almost perverse. In one sense, this popularity was part of a widespread and rather creepy nineteenth-century sentimentalizing of death, something that has been explained in various ways.

In another sense, however, as Stowe's biographer Joan D. Hedrick explains (citing earlier writers, including Nina Baym), the phenomenon was partly in response to a *decrease* in infant mortality: Middle-class parents had begun to invest more emotion in their young children when there began to be a greater likelihood that they would survive infancy. Children began to be regarded as valuable in a new way *as* children and *as* individuals, rather than just as potential adults or even as workers whose efforts would help to support the family. In this new outlook, the child who died (or the child who was sickly and regarded as unlikely to live) became a "special child" (in Baym's and Hedrick's phrase): He or she was seen as a gift sent from God, perhaps a messenger, not meant to live long but intended to have a specific impact on the lives of others. Such a belief, as Hedrick and Baym point out, must have been of great comfort to bereaved parents, and it is this kind of child whose death is celebrated in popular literature.

This "special child" is portrayed in *Uncle Tom's Cabin* as Eva (Evangeline, an angel or heavenly "messenger"). Eva's illness and eventual death do not *cause* her effect upon others, for Eva inspires love in everyone around her (except perhaps for her mother, whose narcissism is so complete that she is unable to love anyone else) even before she falls ill. Her mortal illness is simply a signal of her specialness, inevitably following other signals such as her sometimes un-childlike seriousness and her deep unhappiness at the unhappiness of others. We are supposed to recognize that, as Tom will tell Mammy, the Lord has marked Eva as His own.

Literary Device

Moreover, as a "special child" in the context of popular sentiment, Eva is also special in the specific context of this novel. She is "The Little Evangelist" whose work in this world is to spread the message of love (the message of the New Testament, the message of Christ) in regard to slavery, which both generally and particularly is a sin against love. Eva has told Tom that she wishes she could give her life for slaves, whose own lives are made so unhappy by their condition. In the sense that her life has a special purpose, she is indeed giving it for that purpose, as Tom will give his. Inasmuch as Eva is a symbolic figure in the book, she serves as a figure for love and sacrifice. She is a Christ-figure (as John the Baptist in the New Testament foreshadows Jesus), for Eva's giving of herself precedes and signals Tom's giving of himself.

In these four chapters, too, Eva is one of four very different child characters whose interrelationship is thematically significant. The two girls, Eva and Topsy, are (as dramatists and illustrators have always seen) almost emblematic of an ironic difference between southern children of slavery, a difference that is presented less dramatically (and perhaps more realistically) in the opposition of the two young boys, Dodo and Henrique. The opposition represented by Eva and Topsy is strikingly obvious. Here are two young, pre-adolescent girls, living in the same household. One, Eva, is the only child of the head of the household, pampered and spoiled, given the best education money can afford (we assume; this is never shown), loved lavishly by everyone around her. Eva is indeed a member of one of the first generations of children so singled out for affection and attention, a new kind of child for whom the odds of living past infancy are greater than ever before. The other little girl, Topsy, is nothing that Eva is, has nothing that she has. She does not remember her parents, does not even realize that she had parents. Far from being an only child, she was bred and raised among a herd of children like a farm animal. Instead of being pampered, she was beaten; instead of being taught, she was put to work. She has never been loved. The cause of this almost polar distance between the two girls is slavery; the emblem of the distance is their skin color. Little wonder, then, that "Topsy and Eva" became nearly a standard motif in white American myth, Eva pale and delicate with fine, golden hair (transformed from "honey brown" as Eva's hair is described in the novel), Topsy sturdy and black as coal. Little wonder that the mythical Topsy became a happy, comic child.

Theme

The opposition presented by the characters of Topsy and Eva was real, common, and accepted by the proponents of slavery. An earlier generation, for whom their own children were little more than potential inheritors of their parents' wealth, charged with carrying on the family name (or, among middle and lower economic classes, potential supporters of their aged parents), might understandably have regarded the children of slaves, who were after all merely objects, simply as smaller objects. But how, Stowe seems to ask, can people who love and honor their own children show such dishonor, such failure of love, to these others? The question thus presented by Topsy and Eva is central to this book. One result of the situation illustrated by these two girls is Topsy's moral ignorance, her possible choosing of evil over good (as old Prue chose rather to go to hell than literally to *serve* in heaven). Another possible result is illustrated by Marie: the child who sees herself thus unreasonably favored may, reasonably enough, conclude that she is of supreme worth.

Unfortunately, Stowe could not show this danger to Eva realistically; rather than let this beloved child run the very real risk of growing up like her mother, the writer allowed her little heroine to be touched by God as a special child whose specialness was shown in her love for the injured and oppressed. Worse, Stowe could not even show Topsy as she was likely to have been, had this been a realistic portrait; for sad and ignorant as Topsy is, she is endowed with a spark of energy and resistance that must have been very rare among such. Nor is Topsy incorrigible; a word of love from saintly Eva is all it takes to change Topsy's direction.

More realistic is the same opposition as it is portrayed in the two boys Henrique and Dodo. Both handsome, intelligent, bright children, one is beginning to learn that he may safely use the other as an outlet for his frustrations and treat him, on a personal, physical level, worse than he would be allowed to treat a dog or a horse. The other is beginning to learn that his own feelings, his individuality, the potential that he is aware of within himself, are worth nothing at all in the world he is destined to inhabit.

Glossary

"The grass withereth—the flower fadeth" *Isaiah* 40: 6–8: "A voice says, 'Cry!' / And I said, 'What shall I cry?' / All flesh is grass, / and all its beauty is like the flower of the field. / The grass withers, the flower fades, / when the breath of the LORD blows upon it; / surely the people is grass. / The grass withers, the flower fades; / but the word of our God will stand for ever."

literary cabinet i.e., a bookcase, and, by extension, its contents; Tom's "only literary cabinet" is his Bible.

"one who had 'learned in whatsoever state . . . .'" *Philippians* 4: 11: "I have learned, in whatsoever state I am, therewith to be content."

"that soft, insidious disease" i.e., tuberculosis.

spirituelle (French: *spirituel*) showing a refined nature.

canaille (French) the mob, rabble; a term of contempt for the common people.

St. Domingo the present-day island of Hispaniola; a slave rebellion there resulted in the formation of the country of Haiti.

sans culottes (French: literally, "without breeches") revolutionaries; a term of contempt applied by French aristocrats to the poorly equipped members of the French Revolutionary army, who substituted pantaloons for knee-breeches.

Chapters XXVI–XXVIII
Death; "This Is the Last of Earth"; Reunion

Summary

Eva lies longer in bed each day, her strength fading. Topsy brings Eva a bouquet of flowers, and when Marie tries to keep Topsy out of the room, Eva challenges her mother and takes the flowers. Eva tries to make her mother see that Topsy and the other slaves are children of God, but Marie isn't interested. Eva then asks Ophelia to cut off some locks of Eva's hair, which she distributes among the servants, telling them she will wait to see them in heaven. Eva speaks to her father, trying to get him to say he is a Christian, but although St. Clare recognizes the saintliness of his child, he has no such feeling in himself. Tom spends as much time as possible with Eva, but Mammy must steal opportunities to see her because of Marie's demands. At last St. Clare becomes resigned to Eva's death. Tom begins to sleep on the verandah outside Eva's room and tells Ophelia that he expects death to come soon. When it does come, Tom says, to such a child, all who are watching will have a glimpse of heaven. That night at midnight, Ophelia sees a change come over Eva and calls for the doctor. Eva speaks once to her father; then, as she is dying, he asks her what she sees, and she answers, "O! love,—joy—, peace!"

When Eva's body lies in state in her bedroom, Topsy tries to come in and Rosa sends her away, but St. Clare corrects this, and Topsy throws herself weeping on the floor beside the bed. Ophelia comes in, tries to comfort Topsy, and at last lifts the little girl up and takes her out. St. Clare, recognizing Eva's influence, thinks his own life of little account. Marie's grief is uncontrolled, and she monopolizes the servants. She believes her husband cold; Tom knows better and stays close to St. Clare. The family and servants go back to New Orleans, and St. Clare spends as much time as he can away from home in the cafes and attending to business.

As the weeks go by, St. Clare struggles to find faith and seeks solace in Eva's Bible. He remembers his promise to Eva and begins the legal proceedings to emancipate Tom. Marie continues to be demanding of her servants; Ophelia has become gentler, especially with Topsy, toward whom she no longer feels aversion. She asks that St. Clare immediately sign Topsy over to her legally, and he agrees and gives the girl to Ophelia, who tells St. Clare that the child no more "belongs" to her than she did before; it is only that now she can protect her. She asks if St. Clare has made provisions for his servants in case of his death, and he says he has not.

In a reflective mood, St. Clare plays a piece of religious music on the piano; this surprises and touches Tom and Ophelia. St. Clare and Ophelia talk about Christianity, which he has shunned in part because he believes that most so-called Christians he has known are hypocrites. They talk again about slavery and the inevitability of emancipation, and St. Clare says that the North as well as the South must participate, when that happens, in educating the free men and women and preparing them for self-sufficiency. At that point St. Clare goes out for a walk, and Tom awaits his return. But St. Clare is carried home; he has been stabbed while trying to stop a fight between two men in a café, and he is bleeding to death. A doctor comes; the family and servants gather around in grief and terror. St. Clare begs Tom to pray, and Tom does so. At last St. Clare opens his eyes, says his mother's name, and dies.

Commentary

Eva's death has been well prepared for; we have seen it coming for four chapters at least (and longer than that, if we recognized the signs of her "specialness"). St. Clare's death, too, has been foreshadowed: Eva has told him, in Chapter XXIV, that he will "come to her"; even Ophelia may have had a premonition, causing her to insist on Topsy's becoming her property immediately (for, as an unmarried woman, Ophelia can own property—including this human property—in her own name); and surely St. Clare's thoughts of his mother, on his last afternoon, are feelings of foreboding. Yet this second death is a surprise, at least to his wife and to his servants, who now belong to Marie. No wonder they all weep so pitifully!

Theme

Augustine St. Clare's unexpected death serves, again, to reinforce the theme of moral wrong. If St. Clare was the most generous of masters, indulgent, kind, and actually (sometimes) respectful of his servants as fellow human beings, still his leaving them in other hands, probably worse hands than his, possibly many, many times worse (and we shall see how some of them fare), makes him as bad as those who will now own them. As Haley told young George Shelby, everyone who participates in the business of slavery is reduced to the same level; ironically, St. Clare, the "man of humanity" who has dominated Tom's life for over two years, was no better than the almost demonic figure who will come to own Tom next.

Character
Insight

St. Clare's death serves the novel's plot as well as its theme, allowing Tom to move (as he always moves: by his own Christian will, at the command of others) into a final phase of testing. Always, we have seen Tom's spiritual being and values in tension with the materialism of his masters: Shelby, who sold Tom to pay off debts incurred in market speculation and who benefited from the sale only because Tom elected to fulfill the bargain rather than run away; Haley, to whom any human being is valuable only insofar as he himself can somehow profit and who used Tom's Christian faith as a selling point in his pitch to St. Clare; and then St. Clare himself, whose long materialism, reinforced by his unhappy marriage, is shaken by his daughter's death and then conquered at last by Tom's faith and courageous love. It is ironic that St. Clare was about to free Tom and to send him back to Kentucky when he met his untimely end. Characteristically, Tom's prayer for his master's soul, as the man is dying, contains no hint of bitterness, no consciousness even, that all may be lost now. We know this because his prayer was so pure and powerful that it succeeded.

Theme

But if St. Clare's death is necessary both to the forwarding of the plot and to the theme of slavery's deep moral wrong, it is Eva's death that figures in the novel's larger theme, the redemptive power of Christian faith. Without *her death*, St. Clare would not have been swayed even to curiosity about religion; his experience of Christians is that they are hypocrites (we are reminded of what he told Marie: that if slavery became unprofitable, the churches would turn against it, just as they now find scripture to justify it), and at the same time (he tells Ophelia) he has sensed that real Christianity would demand complete commitment, a commitment he feared he could not give (as of course he could not, at least not believably enough for fiction, given the opposition he would have faced in the person of Marie). But Eva's illness and death leave a great void in St. Clare's life, her Bible comforts him simply because it *is* her Bible, and Tom (guided by God's grace, as he would say and as Stowe would wish us to believe) takes advantage of the situation to stay close to St. Clare and to attempt to bring his master to salvation.

Just before St. Clare is brought home, Tom has slept and dreamed of Eva; he will see her again, in another moment of crisis, and the vision will strengthen him. Thus Eva continues, after death, not only to contribute to the book's theme but also actually to influence the plot, and it is the dead Eva (or at least the dying Eva, more than the living, healthy child) who becomes a mythic figure. In some of the popular nineteenth-century dramatic productions based on *Uncle Tom's Cabin*, the figure of Eva, robed and winged as an angel, presided over the climactic scenes following her death, suspended on wires from the flies. Thematically and mythically, Eva is inseparable from her death.

Glossary

"This is the Last of Earth"   allusion to John Quincy Adams (1767–1848), sixth president of the United States; reportedly his last words were "This is the last of Earth! . . . I am content."

"the long, sacred rest . . . beloved'"   See *Psalms* 127: 2: "It is vain that you rise up early and go late to rest, / eating the bread of anxious toil; / for he gives to his beloved sleep."

"Lord, I believe; help thou my unbelief"   *Mark* 9: 24.

bark   a small sailing boat; figuratively, Eva's life.

ciphers   things of no importance; nonentities.

Moore, Byron, Goethe   Thomas Moore (1779–1852), Irish poet; George Gordon (Lord) Byron (1788–1824), British poet; Johann Wolfgang von Goethe (1749–1832), German poet and dramatist; here, these three are examples of writers who understood religious feeling although they were popularly supposed not to be religious.

exactions   demands, specific requirements.

"In the midst of life we are in death"   line from the Burial of the Dead in the *Book of Common Prayer*.

"When the Son of man . . . . As ye did it not to one of the least of these . . . ."   *Matthew* 25: 31–46.

Chapters XXIX–XXXII
The Unprotected; The Slave Warehouse; The Middle Passage; Dark Places

Summary

At St. Clare's death, the servants are all terrified, because they are well acquainted with Marie, who now has complete control over their lives. Their terror is justified, as Rosa soon finds, when she talks back to Marie and is ordered to go to a whipping-establishment. Rosa pleads with Ophelia to intervene with Marie on her behalf, for she and Ophelia both know that young women sent to one of these places will be raped. Ophelia tries to make Marie change her mind, but Marie will not. A few days later, Marie decides to sell the New Orleans house, furniture, and slaves, and return to her parents' house. At Tom's request, Ophelia asks Marie to give him his freedom, as St. Clare had promised, but to no avail. The next day, Tom, Adolph, and several others are taken to a slave warehouse to await their sale.

In Chapter XXX, Tom, Adolph, and a number of other slaves await sale in a warehouse. A large slave tries to bully Tom without success; he does better with Adolph, whom he calls a "white nigger." Adolph tries to fight this man, and the white keeper parts them. In the women's quarters, two of the female slaves are Susan and Emmeline, mother and daughter. The mother, Susan, fears that 15-year-old Emmeline will be sold as a sex slave and tells her to comb her hair back and try to look as plain as possible.

The next morning, the sale commences. Adolph is sold to a young man who wants a valet and has said he will teach Adolph his place. Tom and Emmeline (separated from her mother) are sold to a revolting man who had earlier inspected them, as are two other men. They now belong to a Mr. Legree, the owner of a cotton plantation.

In Chapter XXXI, as they travel to the Legree plantation, Tom realizes that he is in the worst of hands. Legree throws some of Tom's belongings (including his hymnal) into the river and then sells Tom's trunk and its contents to the boat-hands. Legree paws Emmeline, telling her she'd better be pleasant when he talks to her. Then he shows his new slaves his fist, saying it got so hard from knocking down slaves. Later, in the boat's bar, he brags to the other white men about his treatment of slaves, saying he feels it is cheaper in the long run to use them up and buy more than it is to take care of them with good food, medicine, and so on.

In Chapter XXXII, the journey to Legree's plantation continues, through rough country, in a wagon. Legree orders the slaves to sing, but when Tom starts a hymn, he tells him to shut up. Another man begins a foolish, meaningless song, and the others join in. The narrator tells us that it is the only way these men can express their sorrow or pray, for the master hears only what he thinks is noisy good humor. Legree is drinking, and he paws the frightened Emmeline, obviously anxious to get home with her.

They get to the plantation house, once a fine, well-kept mansion but now a wreck among ruined grounds. Two black men, Sambo and Quimbo, Legree's overseers, come to greet the wagon with several dogs, and Legree tells the newcomers they had better behave, for the dogs would be happy to eat them. Legree presents Sambo with the older woman he has just acquired, saying he has promised to bring him a woman; when Lucy (as her name is) protests that she has a husband, Legree tells her to shut up. He takes Emmeline into the house, and Tom sees a woman's face at the window and hears an angry voice, with Legree responding that he'll do as he likes. Tom is taken to a crude shanty without furniture, and Sambo tells him he may sleep there, not in private, as Tom had hoped, but with many others.

Late in the evening, the slaves return from the fields and must grind, mix, and bake their dried corn over an open fire for their supper. The strongest go first, for these slaves are so desperate that they show no regard for each other. Sambo tries to make Lucy grind his corn and cook his supper, and she says she would rather die than live as his woman. Tom waits until very late to get access to a mill, and then he grinds corn and builds up the fire for two weary women. After their meager meal, the women go to their huts, and Tom sits by the fire; he feels his faith tested by his hardships. He goes back then to his hut and finds that the floor is covered with sleeping men. He is cold and tired, so he wraps himself with a ragged blanket and sleeps. He dreams that Eva is reading to him from the Bible, and he wakes comforted.

Commentary

In Chapter XXIX, we see the effects of St. Clare's failure to carry out Eva's wishes and free his slaves, for by his death they have passed into the hands of his wife, Marie, who now has complete control over their lives. St. Clare, as he told his cousin Ophelia, had made no will, at least none that decided the fate of the human beings he "owned"—and probably none at all. Now Tom and the rest are at Marie's mercy. We see that St. Clare's "kindness" to his slaves—his indulgence of Adolph's thievery, his refusal to allow Marie to have them whipped—has had an effect opposite what he intended, for Rosa's quick temper (her habit of speaking unguardedly, like a free woman) has allowed Marie to do what she has no doubt always wished to do, for Rosa is a pretty woman and Marie has faded.

Theme

Rosa's punishment—sexual abuse by a paid brutalizer of slaves—exemplifies what the narrator has told us, at the opening of Chapter XXIX, about the corrupting influence of the slaveowner's power. The two women involved here, Rosa and Marie, are both basically thoughtless, shallow, more interested in fashion than anything else. In other words, they are typical products of their culture, unredeemed by real religion or depth of emotion. Slavery has shaped them both, using Rosa as an object, semi-decorative, rather like a household appliance, and convincing Marie that she is the center of the universe. Now slavery has punished Rosa for her thoughtlessness by subjecting her to shameful harm, perhaps ruining her life, certainly changing her already-degraded life for the worse; and it has turned Marie into a monster who can order the rape of a young woman for an ostensible reason even she must recognize as trivial. Marie is now, at the end of our acquaintance with her, capable of doing real evil, and she is totally empowered to do so.

Literary Device

In the slave warehouse, we encounter several bitter ironies. Considering its function, the narrator tells us, this ought to be a hellish place in appearance, but instead it looks much like any other house; slavery makes sin—offenses against God, against the good; against love, in this book's terms—just another business, to be conducted genteelly. Here the slaves are supposed to be having a good time while they await sale, for part of the justification of slavery by those who participate in it is that the condition of slavery is proper for these people, and they are happy to be in their proper place. Potential buyers want to believe this, so those who run the warehouse encourage (and enforce, if necessary) the appearance of carefree happiness in order to increase their own profit. Similarly, the young girl Emmeline, so innocent that she doesn't understand her mother's fears for her (believably so, for a 15-year-old could be protected from sexual experience and knowledge in the 1850s—probably even a 15-year-old slave girl, if her mother was vigilant and her owner compliant), is forced to advertise her own sexual attractiveness in order to increase the warehouse-owner's profit.

Within one of the embedded narratives of this section (the other being the story of Lucy, taken from her husband without his knowledge and sold to Legree), we find another irony—a common one, it is implied. Susan and Emmeline, who belonged to a widow, were part of an estate mismanaged by its inheritor, their former owner's son. Thus they are now in the hands of a New York firm whose lawyers are having them sold. While it is illegal for residents of New York to own slaves, it is of course not illegal for such business to be conducted.

Theme

Here, more strongly than in the other instances where the overpowering interests of capital are cited, the narrator pinpoints the reason why slavery continues: Although one of the New York partners is said to be uneasy about allowing this sale of human beings as part of his transaction, his firm would lose $30,000 (in today's figures, perhaps 20 times that much) by refusing the transaction. It is simply too much money for a businessman to sacrifice on principle, and so Emmeline will be sold to a man who intends to use her sexually until he tires of her. The point is this: The business and political decisions of the country (including the continuation of slavery) are made by men who are trained—despite the fact they may nominally be Christian—to ignore what they know to be right (emotional knowledge, which is thus "feminine" and rejected) in favor of what they know to be profitable. The New York businessman, in capitulating to the sale of slaves, makes essentially the same decision that was made by the Ohio senator, Bird: one in favor of "larger interests" than morality.

We see also, in the slave warehouse, the human irony of Adolph, formerly the manager of St. Clare's household, who as we have seen had some difficulty distinguishing between his belongings and his master's. St. Clare seems to have encouraged Adolph's habitual dishonesty, much as he encouraged Rosa's quick temper, through a combination of laziness and guilt; as he told Ophelia, he felt he could not blame slaves for stealing—he himself, had he been in their position, would probably have done the same. But Adolph, like Jane and Rosa, having enjoyed a relatively high status both in the St. Clare household and in the New Orleans community (and having, perhaps understandably, lorded it over others whose status was not so high), had all the farther to fall when St. Clare died. Racial slavery has taught Adolph that his African ancestry is far less valuable than his European ancestry; he has been rewarded for admiring St. Clare and emulating him. Now, like the cook, Dinah, who reminded Adolph that he was finally no better off than she, the other slaves in the warehouse, lower in social status (and darker-skinned), resent the arrogance that Adolph seems by his very appearance to assume, and they harass him for it. Having no sense of his own worth *within himself,* he tries to fight his chief tormenter (a fight he would probably lose), but although the "keeper" stops the two men, Adolph has no friends here but Tom. Nor will he have a friend in his next master, who recognizes Adolph's usefulness (his intelligence and "cultivation") but voices his intent to break Adolph's independent spirit.

Character Insight

The characters Adolph, Rosa, and Jane have not been drawn sympathetically; but they are—like most of the minor characters in this novel—relatively complex and realistic portrayals. These three characters are young adults who have been given no encouragement or help to rise above their material human condition. They are vain, frivolous, selfish, cruel (specifically to Dinah and Topsy) without their cruelty being particularly effective, dishonest in smallish ways, and ignorant. They have no religion. The only person to take them seriously and urge them to live up to their human potential (by prayer)—the only person really to believe in them as children of God—is Eva.

Later, after Eva's death, Ophelia tries to follow the lead of the child; and Tom, of course, although his interactions with them are not described, must also have treated them with real kindness and respect. Adolph and Rosa, at least, are shown to repay Ophelia and Tom with trust and good will, as they have given Eva their true grief. Now, after St. Clare's death, we hear no more of Jane, but we see both Rosa and Adolph suffering terrible fates. More than the very minor figures of the embedded narratives, whose sufferings stun us momentarily, time after time—perhaps even more than Tom, whose sacrifice is of his own choosing (every time he renews his Christian commitment) and is redemptive—Rosa and Adolph seem to embody slavery's true horror, its insult to the humanity of ordinary people whom it first degrades, treats as objects until they begin to believe they are only objects, and then punishes for their degradation.

On the other side of slavery, of course, are people like St. Clare, who is himself degraded by slavery although he believes himself to be acting humanely within a system he inherited. But in this section, we are introduced to a character who has actively chosen degradation—for himself and for the people whom he buys, uses up, and takes pride as well as perverse pleasure from turning into objects without respect for themselves or each other. Simon Legree, Tom's new master, is portrayed in depth as a horrifying human being—not, like Haley, a mere materialist, caring only for profit (and not, like Shelby, dismissing the equal humanity of slaves), but a morally and spiritually warped individual who will, if need be, sacrifice even profit to exercise the full power of pain and evil over other human beings under his sway. Legree obviously does *not* subscribe to any of the racist theories by which other slaveowners may justify their use of human beings for economic gain; he must be fully aware of his slaves' equal human potential in order to enjoy their degradation. As the novel takes us up the Red River on the steamboat *Pirate,* through a wasteland of swamps and barrens, toward the decaying mansion and hopeless shanties of Legree's plantation, we enter the truly Gothic heart of darkness presided over by this truly Gothic villain.

Glossary

"He that dwelleth in love . . . ." *1 John* 4:16: "So we know and believe the love God has for us. God is love, and he who abides in love abides in God, and God abides in him."

Tartarus "informis, ingens, cui lumen ademptum" Latin: Hell, "misshapen, monstrous, devoid of light."

toilet i.e., the process of dressing and grooming oneself.

palmetto a hat woven of palmetto leaves.

rattan a cane or switch made from a branch of rattan (a kind of palm tree).

exquisite a person who makes a show of being refined and fastidious in matters of taste, etc.; a dandy.

calaboose [Old Slang] a prison; jail; here, a whipping-establishment or specific place for punishment of slaves.

lot one's portion in life; fortune; fate (in the sense of its being decided by chance).

saloon   any large room designed for entertainments, receptions, etc.

stock   a former type of large, wide, stiff cravat (necktie); here, apparently, Legree uses the word to mean Tom's necktie or scarf.

"what's yer name"   i.e., "what's-your-name," a belittling form of address directed at a person whose name the speaker does not (or pretends not to) know.

"Fear not! for I have redeemed thee . . . ."   *Isaiah* 43: 1: "But now thus says the Lord, / he who created you, O Jacob, / he who formed you, O Israel: 'Fear not, for I have redeemed you; / I have called you by name, you are mine.'"

"The dark places of the earth . . . ."   *Psalms* 74: 20, 21: "Have regard for thy covenant; / for the dark places of the land are full of the habitations of violence. / Let not the downtrodden be put to shame; / let the poor and needy praise thy name."

barrens   places that do not produce useful crops or fruits; places with poor soil; here, "pine barrens" are woods whose plants are chiefly or overwhelmingly pine trees.

peck   a unit of dry measure, equal to a quarter of a bushel or 8 dry quarts.

"Come unto ME, all ye . . . ."   *Matthew* 11: 28: "Come unto me, all ye that labor and are heavy laden, and I will give you rest. / Take my yoke upon you, and learn of me; for I am meek and lowly in heart: and ye shall find rest unto your souls. / For my yoke is easy, and my burden is light."

"When thou passest through the waters, . . . "   *Isaiah* 43: 2, 3: "'When you pass through the waters I will be with you; / and through the rivers, they shall not overwhelm you; / when you walk through fire you shall not be burned, / and the flame shall not consume you. / For I am the Lord your God, / the Holy One of Israel, your Savior.'"

Chapters XXXIII–XXXVI
Cassy; The Quadroon's Story; The Tokens; Emmeline and Cassy

Summary

Tom soon becomes familiar with what is expected of him on Legree's plantation. He is quiet, diligent, and—despite his disgust with what he sees—trusting in God and hopeful of somehow escaping this life. Legree hates him, for he recognizes Tom's moral superiority and sees that he cannot be manipulated. So Legree determines to break Tom's spirit.

One morning a strange woman appears in the field, working alongside Tom. The others jeer at her for having to work, saying they hope to see her flogged, but she works easily and efficiently. That same day, Lucy is obviously ill and in need of help, so Tom puts some of the cotton from his sack into hers. Sambo, overseeing them, kicks and abuses Lucy, and as soon as he turns away, Tom gives her all of his cotton. She protests, saying he'll be punished for this, and he replies that he is more able to stand that than she is. The strange woman, hearing this, gives Tom some of the cotton from *her* sack but tells him that he doesn't know the place; in a month, he will not be so kind.

That evening, Sambo tells Legree that Tom is helping Lucy and will cause trouble with the others. Legree tells his overseers that they will have to break Tom in. On the pretext that Lucy's cotton basket is underweight, Legree orders Tom to flog her; Tom refuses. Legree loses his temper and asks if Tom does not belong to him, body and soul. To this, Tom replies that Legree has bought his body but could never own his soul and says that Legree can't harm him. Legree gives Tom to Sambo and Quimbo to be punished.

In Chapter XXXIV, Tom, injured and bleeding, lies alone in the gin-house, trying to pray. The strange woman from the field, Cassy, gives him water and dresses his wounds. She tells him he has been brave but that he must now give up; there is no God, she says, or if there is, He is set against them. The other slaves, she says, are not worth his suffering; they would turn against him in a minute. Tom says he has lost everything else, and he refuses to lose his soul. She tells Tom he will be tortured to death if he does not give up his resistance to Legree, and he replies that he will be dead then and beyond hurting. Then Cassy, thinking of Emmeline, tells Tom her own story.

In Chapter XXXV, Legree sits in his cluttered house, drinking punch and regretting having let Sambo talk him into punishing Tom, who now is unfit to work. Cassy hears him and sneers at him; she reminds him that he fears her, and with reason. The narrator tells us that Cassy has a sexual hold over Legree, but that he also fears her because he suspects she is insane, which in his superstitious mind amounts to possession. Cassy has taken Emmeline's side against him and has worked in the field for a day to prove to him that she doesn't fear his threat to send her there. Legree admits that he was foolish to have Tom whipped so severely but says he is determined to break Tom's spirit. Just then Sambo comes in with something he has found while flogging Tom; he says this is a charm Tom wears against feeling pain. Actually, it is the silver dollar given Tom by young George Shelby, together with the lock of Eva's hair. The lock of hair curls around Legree's finger and he screams in fear, throwing the thing into the fire. At this point Cassy goes out to tend Tom—the action of the previous chapter.

The narrator explains what has troubled Legree. It seems that he was well brought up in New England, by a kind, Christian mother, but he turned against her and went to sea, leading a life of depravity. His mother continued to pray for him, but when he next saw her he cursed her, choosing his sinful life once and for all. Soon he received a letter telling him of his mother's death and containing a lock of her hair. He was horrified, burning the hair and living in dread of his mother's ghost. Now, not knowing whose hair Tom had kept, he feared it as his mother's hair. His house begins to frighten him, and he tries to rouse Emmeline. She will not answer, however, and he is afraid to go upstairs after her. He starts up, but hears Emmeline singing about the Last Judgment; in fear and horror, he goes back downstairs. At last he calls in Sambo and Quimbo, and the three get drunk together; Cassy, returning, looks in at them and wonders if it would be sinful to kill Legree. She then goes upstairs to call upon Emmeline.

In Chapter XXXIV, Emmeline is sitting up, frightened of the noise of the drunken men downstairs. She asks Cassy if they couldn't escape, but Cassy tells her this has been tried; even if one could survive in the swamps that surround the plantation, the dogs would find her. She implies that Legree has had would-be escapees burned at the stake. She tells Emmeline that the best thing for her would be to drink Legree's brandy, which would make it easier for her to give in to him—something she apparently has not yet done. (How Emmeline has managed to avoid Legree's advances so far is not explained, but one might infer that he wants to force her *willing* compliance, rather than simply rape her; also, it is implied that he is afraid of Cassy in this regard, as well as in other matters.)

In the morning, Legree wakes from a night of horrible dreams. Cassy comes into the room and tells him he had better leave Tom alone. She says she's done what she could for Tom; Legree paid $1,200 for him, she reminds him, and he ought to be more careful of his property. Legree sees the wisdom of this but says Tom will have to beg his forgiveness. Legree goes to see Tom, kicks him, and orders him to get on his knees and beg pardon. Tom refuses, saying he will do whatever work Legree orders but will not do what he knows to be wrong, though he be killed for refusing. Legree flies into a rage and knocks Tom down with his fist, but Cassy comes up behind him, and he remembers his fears of the previous night. Saying that he will break Tom eventually, Legree leaves. Cassy tells Tom that, now he has won Legree's ill will, the man will dog him until he has bled him dry.

Commentary

An early critic of the novel, Martin Delany (writing in 1853), suggested that a really heroic slave protagonist, unlike Tom, would have killed his master rather than have allowed him to accomplish his evil domination. This complaint is a traditional one against Tom and against the book itself; the phrase "Uncle Tom" has become a term of contempt, defined in *Webster's New World College Dictionary* as "a black whose behavior toward whites is regarded as fawning or servile."

Of course, had the fictional circumstances been slightly different—had George Harris been sold south, eventually to wind up on Legree's plantation—we know from George's response to his previous servitude and to Tom Loker's pursuit that he might have behaved in a way more acceptable to such critics as Delany; in fact, George's refusal to accept slavery and its laws is a response which Harriet Beecher Stowe imagined, approved, and rewarded (as shall be seen). But her central hero, Tom, is possessed of a strength that Stowe regarded as being of a higher order than George's strength: the strength of a true Christian (whereas George, originally unable to accept Christianity, originally in fact doubting the existence or at least the goodness of God, must be led by Eliza's faith and the help of the Quaker Simeon Halliday to believe at last in God's presence and eventual justice). Tom, while agreeing with his wife that forgiveness of one's persecutors is not *natural*, argued that God's grace enables one to overcome nature; this is exactly what Tom is able to do.

Theme

The theme of Christian passivity is not an easy one to accept, especially not in fiction, perhaps, when one would prefer to see a protagonist prevail physically against such a horrid antagonist as Simon Legree. But if the underlying conflict of the book is the battle of goodness against evil—specifically the evil of slavery, which functions by objectifying human beings, turning them into things—then goodness, personified in Tom himself, must prevail by refusing this objectification. This is what Tom does when he refuses to allow Legree to corrupt him, saying he absolutely will not do what he knows to be wrong. Those who say that Tom ought to have killed Legree argue a situational ethic (murder is generally wrong, but in this situation it would be right, since this person is likely to do serious wrongs in the future). In fact, that is what Cassy considers doing at the end of Chapter XXXV. But although to have Tom kill Legree (or to have Cassy kill him and save Tom the trouble) might have been a satisfying solution in some readers' minds, it misses the point. Tom cannot prevail over Legree by killing him but only by refusing to be *used* by him as an implement of Legree's evil. If Legree is able to *make* Tom do anything that Tom knows is wrong—even the murder of Legree himself—then evil, not good (objectification, not love, in this book's terms), has prevailed.

Nor is Tom's refusal the act of an "Uncle Tom" as the dictionary defines the term—a black sycophant to whites, a servile flatterer, a collaborator. Early in the novel, when Chloe urges Tom to run away (after learning that Shelby has sold him to Haley), Tom's refusal is based on the knowledge that, unless he satisfies Shelby's bargain, the entire estate—including its slaves, his wife and children among them—must be sold. Again, on Legree's plantation, Tom willingly accepts punishment rather than inflict punishment on another slave, Lucy. He *refuses* to be servile, a collaborator against his fellows—a role that Legree's two overseers have been forced and coerced into playing.

Character Insight

One of the most interesting characters in the book, appearing in this late section, is the woman Cassy, Legree's unwilling mistress, whose strength is related to her femininity in a more traditional sense. Cassy's sexual power over Legree is reinforced by his superstitious fear of her—a combination that seems also to have its effect upon the overseer

Sambo and perhaps upon the other slaves in the field, who seem to resent this strangely beautiful woman but keep their distance from her. Sandra Gilbert and Susan Gubar, in a critical work entitled *The Madwoman in the Attic* (1979), argue that Cassy turns a conventional Gothic female character (personified by "Bertha Mason" in Charlotte Brontë's *Jane Eyre*) on its head. Certainly Cassy combines the sexual strength and vulnerability, along with the hint of dangerous madness, that defines many a Gothic heroine, and we shall see how she uses all of this to her advantage.

In the meantime, Cassy's story—one of the most developed of the book's embedded narratives, narrated by Cassy herself—interrupts the scene of Tom's suffering with another tale of suffering. Cassy's career of sexual slavery began, ironically, with a relationship that the young teenager believed was a marriage; she was sold by her "husband" to pay off gambling debts, incurred—again ironically—as a result of influence by a "friend" whose aim was to secure Cassy for himself. Cassy has already committed murder once; a justified homicide, she believes, for she killed her young infant to save it from a fate similar to that of her two other children, Henri (whom she saw for the last time as he was being beaten in a whipping establishment) and Elise, whom she believes was sold into sexual slavery. Cassy has attempted another murder, of the man who betrayed her "husband" and sold her children, and she is now considering the murder of Simon Legree. Perhaps Legree knows of her history of killing and knows that this act is said to become easier with practice. At any rate, he may be in control of whatever else happens on his plantation, but he is, to a certain extent, under Cassy's control.

Character Insight

But only to a certain extent—for Cassy knows Legree, knows how evil he is, and knows what he is capable of. Josephine Donovan (*"Uncle Tom's Cabin": Evil, Affliction, and Redemptive Love,* 1991) argues that Legree represents the worst of the book's materialists, a personification of the profit motive taken to its extreme. Indeed, this is an accurate reading of Legree as a character; but, unlike Haley, whom Shelby described for his wife as someone who would sell his own old mother without blinking, Legree knows exactly what his devotion to profit means, has chosen it freely (in rejecting his mother and her prayers), and is in love with it to the ruin of himself and everyone over whom he has power. One passage from the New Testament that Stowe does *not* have her characters or narrator quote, but that she must have been aware of as it applies to Legree, is *I Timothy*, 6:10: "For the love of money is the root of all evils . . . ." Legree's love of profit, which may have begun in him as innocently as it began in any of this book's characters (for example Shelby, whose unlucky investments in the market forced his sale of Tom and little Harry), has progressed into an insatiable hunger. Cassy characterizes him correctly, at the end of Chapter XXXVI, as that direst of Gothic monsters, a vampire.

Glossary

camphire   i.e., camphor, a chemical compound with a strong characteristic odor; as spirits of camphor, often used as a stimulant.

"Servants, obey your masters"   *Ephesians* 6: 5: "Slaves, be obedient to those who are your earthly masters, with fear and trembling, in singleness of heart, as to Christ . . . ."; (see also *Titus* 2: 9: "Bid slaves to be submissive to their masters and to give satisfaction in every respect . . . ."); these passages were frequently cited as New Testament authority for slavery.

gin-house   an outbuilding sheltering the *cotton gin*, a machine for separating cotton fibers from the seeds.

pallaise   a pallet, or thin mattress.

convent   i.e., convent school; a boarding school for girls run by Catholic nuns.

punch   a mixture of alcoholic spirits with water or fruit juice and sugar, often heated.

inly   i.e., inwardly, within one's mind or spirit.

necromancy   black magic; sorcery.

"I am the root and offspring of David, and the bright and morning star"   *Revelation* 22:16: "'I Jesus have sent my angel to you with this testimony for the churches. I am the root and the offspring of David, the bright morning star.'"

Chapters XXXVII–XLI
Liberty; The Victory; The Stratagem; The Martyr; The Young Master

Summary

In Chapter XXXVII, the scene changes to a farmhouse in the Midwest, where the slave-catcher Tom Loker is being cared for by an elderly Quaker woman. Although sullen and bad-tempered, he knows that, if it weren't for the kindness of the fugitives, he would still be lying in the road, and so he reveals that George and Eliza and the others are being watched for in Sandusky (Ohio) and that Eliza should disguise herself. In accordance with Loker's advice, the fugitive party splits up, Eliza dresses like a man, and they dress Harry up like a little girl. In this way, they are able to safely make their crossing into Canada and freedom.

Chapter XXXVIII returns to Legree's plantation, where Tom has gone back to work in the fields long before his wounds are healed. As day after grueling day passes, he becomes more and more discouraged. Tom feels his faith sorely tested, and although he prays, he has begun to feel that prayer is of no help. This is Tom's lowest moment, as he feels his faith slipping away from him. Suddenly, though, he is granted a vision of Christ, and his faith is restored.

One night, Cassy comes to Tom and says she has drugged Legree's brandy and asks him to kill Legree with an axe; she would do it herself, she says, but she feels she hasn't the strength. Tom refuses and tells her she must not kill Legree, for to do so would be to sell her soul to evil. Instead, he encourages her to take Emmeline and run away.

In Chapter XXXIX, we learn that Cassy has been storing provisions as well as clothes for Emmeline and herself in the garret of Legree's house, which is reputedly haunted by the ghost of a slave woman who had died there after being locked up by Legree. Cassy has also arranged some things in the garret to make odd noises when the wind comes through openings. Legree, who is very superstitious, becomes more and more uneasy about the garret, and Cassy continues to encourage this.

When Cassy and Emmeline finally make their escape into the swamp, pursued by Legree and others, the two circle back to the house and hide in the garret. There they plan to stay until Legree has exhausted the search for them in the surrounding country.

Legree's hunt, naturally, is unsuccessful and, believing that Tom knows where the women went, sends Quimbo to drag Tom to him. Tom, although he knows that he is facing death, refuses to tell what he knows about the escape. At Legree's command, Sambo and Quimbo beat Tom until he is nearly dead. Weakly, he says that he forgives Legree; then he faints. After Legree leaves, the two overseers are finally sorry for what they have done. When Tom regains consciousness, he tells them weakly that he forgives them, too, and they both break down and weep.

Chapter XLI sees the arrival of young George Shelby at Legree's estate. He has arrived to buy Tom back, but he has come too late: Tom is dying. George begs Tom to live, but Tom says the Lord is taking him home—and Heaven is better than Kentucky—and he makes George promise not to tell Chloe how he has died. Then, secure in the love of Christ, Tom dies.

Commentary

For a long time, after the early popularity of *Uncle Tom's Cabin* (both with ordinary readers and with critics) had passed and the book was out of critical fashion, its structure was said to be either haphazard or non-existent. Because Stowe had, in a sense, composed as she went along, with the original publication in serial form, it was thought that she had given little thought to its formal structure. More recently, critics have recognized several elements of the book's structure. For example, its geographical movements, from the Shelby farm in Kentucky northward and southward, are seen to be thematically important; and its interruptions of one of the major plots with one or more chapters following the other plot are seen to follow a pattern (which one writer, Elaine Showalter, likens to that of a patchwork quilt; see the Critical Essays).

In the section just summarized, both geographical movement and plot interruption figure as important elements. The contrast between settings and situations is especially ironic, for Chapter XXXVII begins with a wounded man lying in bed, being tended by a woman, the same situation with which the previous chapter ended. But whereas in one case the scene is the dark, hot gin-house on Legree's hellish plantation, where Tom has been left to suffer by all but Cassy, in the other it is a cheerful, bright, relatively cool Midwestern farmhouse where Loker's assurance of recovery is due to the Christian kindness not only of the Quakers but also of the escaped slaves whom he had attempted to capture.

Another contrast is between the characters central to their respective plots. Tom lingers in the hopelessness and motionlessness of his captivity, slowly losing his faith, surrounded by people as hopeless as himself and taunted by his tormentor. Enclosed on all sides by impenetrable swamp, which has been described as full of insects and snakes, he is powerless to escape. In contrast, we see Eliza and her family, now safe in a network of others who will break the law to help them, easily eluding their would-be captors and traveling swiftly north across a great, free body of water into their own new life of freedom. This scene, which is the last glimpse we shall have of the Harris family until later in their lives, is a welcome relief from the atmosphere of the other plot, which has steadily grown more oppressive and hopeless. At the same time, having had this breath of air, this glimpse of freedom, we feel the hellishness of Tom's situation even more strongly when we return to it: After the narrator's introduction to Chapter XXXVIII, that chapter's first scene, with Legree playing the tempter, urging Tom to throw his Bible into the flames, is indeed infernal.

But immediately after we have seen Tom at the nadir of his faith, we are allowed to share his vision of Christ's crown of thorns changed to one of glory. We are reminded that Tom, in the gin-house, asked Cassy to read to him, from the New Testament, the story of the crucifixion. Now, in this vision of the resurrection, the mood of the novel lifts. Just as Tom now feels Legree powerless to hurt him, the reader, too, sees this satanic character somehow dwindling, becoming smaller, even faintly ridiculous, as he engages in silly chatter with his overseers about the fun of catching Tom should he try to escape—and especially as he falls stupidly into Cassy's trap for his superstition. In this section, the novel changes direction: Its climax is not Tom's death but his renewal of faith. After that moment, both Tom and the reader feel that his death is inevitable, and both accept it. But the balance of power has swung from Legree to Tom, and everyone—including Legree—knows it.

Several details of this section call for particular attention. Cassy's determination to kill Legree—the nadir of *her* captivity—comes after Tom has regained his own spiritual equilibrium, and he is able to save her from doing so. There is no question that his concern here is for Cassy herself, rather than for Legree. She *must not* kill the man, Tom tells her, because of the cost to her immortal soul. Tom is speaking (and

Stowe speaks through him) in spiritual terms, but as is so often the case, his point is a psychological one as well. Cassy's life, during which she has been used for sex until she is almost used up, has turned her forcibly away from *love*, and Tom knows this. But, as he also knows, God *is* love; to live in love is to live in God, and to turn away from one is to turn away from the other. To murder Legree would be the ultimate act of turning away, for Cassy, from any possibility for her own happiness.

Instead, what Tom suggests for her is a specific act of love: the attempt to take young Emmeline away from Legree's brutality. Tom knows that the women's actual chances of escaping are very slim—he has no way to see ahead of time what Cassy's plan will be or whether it will succeed. But he knows that death incurred in such a loving act will be infinitely preferable for both women, spiritually and psychologically, to even a long life after killing Legree, which life would be lived in the emptiness of bitter hatred. In his own life, Tom has undoubtedly seen many people whose existence was centered upon bitterness and vengeance—old Prue, in New Orleans, was such a one—and he knows how debilitating this sort of emotion is to people who carry it.

As Tom's new vision, his clarity of faith, has affected Cassy, so too it affects Sambo and Quimbo, the up-to-now nearly demonic henchmen of the devilish Legree. Never characterized in depth, these two have simply been described as men whom Legree uses against each other and his other slaves. Now, when they apparently suddenly turn into Christians after mortally injuring Tom, we may be inclined to disbelief. In fact, however, we may see not only a spiritual but also a psychological validity in Sambo and Quimbo's change of heart, just as there is for Cassy's sudden clarity of mind.

Although we know nothing about these men's lives before their coming into Legree's literal possession, we may assume that Legree selected them for some strength of character as well as physical capabilities; perhaps they both held out against him for nearly as long as Tom did, or perhaps they quickly saw that their only chance for survival was to collaborate with him—as Cassy urged Tom to do, and as Tom, without the strength of his religious faith, might well have done. Still, Sambo and Quimbo have been witness to the dramatic conflict between Tom and Legree, and they—like the others—have seen Tom's recent rise in strength along with Legree's diminishment. At some point, if the situation were allowed to continue, the two overseers themselves would almost certainly have decided to turn against their master and toward

Tom; only the fact that they have been manipulated into conflict with each other has kept them from doing so. It is not so implausible, then, that after their combined violence against Tom has been unsuccessful, and after Legree himself has given up, these two men should at last recognize Tom's superior strength—superior to Legree's strength and superior to their own. And they are bound to recognize that strength's source in Tom's spirit, in his Christian faith. Their "conversion," then, is first of all an acknowledgment of respect for the man himself and beyond that—because of who Tom is—an admission of allegiance to his God.

In a wholly different vein, some readers may find another incident from this section slightly implausible: Eliza's successful disguise as a man, allowing her to escape. True, the ploy of having a young woman pretend to be a man in order to slip through whatever lines she must slip through was used often enough in sentimental literature that we might be forgiven for seeing it as a somewhat unrealistic cliché. After all, we ourselves would never be fooled by such a "disguise": A lovely and very feminine-looking person like Eliza, with her hair cut short and wearing a well-fitted jacket and trousers, would look exactly like what she was—a young lady in a pant-suit. We might not even notice that she was actually dressed in "men's" clothes. But in fact, women in the nineteenth century managed to disguise themselves this way, successfully, with some regularity. In a time when women *never* wore anything faintly resembling "men's" clothing, when they *always* wore waist-pinching corsets, long full skirts, and elaborately artificial hairdos topped by elaborately artificial hats, no one had to look at anything but the costume to determine the gender of the person wearing it. And so, apparently, no one did.

Glossary

"The earth shall be dissolved . . . . / Than when we first begun"
These are verses from the hymn "Amazing Grace."

"What have we to do with thee, thou Jesus . . . ?" *Matthew* 8: 29: "And behold, they cried out, 'What have you to do with us, O Son of God? Have you come here to torment us before the time?'" (The speakers are demons, whom Jesus is about to drive out of two men and into a herd of swine.)

"sift ye as wheat" *Luke* 22: 31: "Simon, Simon, behold, Satan demanded to have you, that he might sift you like wheat . . . " (Jesus, speaking to his disciple Simon Peter, at the Last Supper.)

"a land of darkness and the shadow of death"   *Job* 10: 20–22: "Are not the days of my life few? / Let me alone, that I may find a little comfort / before I go whence I shall not return, / to the land of gloom and deep darkness, / the land of gloom and chaos, / where light is as darkness."

stiletto   a small dagger, having a slender, tapering blade; or, a small, sharp-pointed instrument for making holes in cloth, etc. (Cassy's stiletto might plausibly be either, but the second sense seems more likely.)

flambeaux   (French) lighted torches.

Bryant   i.e., William Cullen Bryant (1794–1878), U.S. poet and journalist.

curveting   making leaps, as in equestrian exhibitions (a *curvet* is a movement where the horse rears, then lifts both back legs into the air just before the front legs come down); here, the implication is that the horses and riders are anxious to be off on the hunt.

"Into thy hands I commend my spirit!"   Jesus' dying words on the cross; see *Luke* 23: 46: "Then Jesus, crying with a loud voice, said, 'Father, into thy hands I commit my spirit!' And having said this he breathed his last."

"instrument of torture"   i.e., the Cross.

Eternal Rock   i.e., Christ, the "Rock of Ages" (see, for example, *I Corinthians* 10: 4: "[A]nd all drank the same supernatural drink. For they drank from the supernatural Rock which followed them, and the Rock was Christ").

Chapters XLII–XLV
An Authentic Ghost Story; Results; The Liberator; Concluding Remarks

Summary

The night after Tom's burial, Legree rides to town, gets drunk, comes home, locks his door, and goes to bed. He wakes to see a ghost standing in the room, beckoning to him, and he faints. On the same night, shortly after Legree sees the ghost, the servants notice that the house door is open, and they see two white figures—actually Cassy and Emmeline—gliding down the lane. Cassy and Emmeline get to the next town, having changed out of their sheets and dressed as a Spanish Creole lady and her servant. Cassy, who has stolen some of Legree's money, buys a trunk and awaits the next riverboat. George Shelby is also waiting, and he and Cassy become acquainted. Cassy takes the young Kentuckian into her confidence when they board the boat, and George tells her he will do what he can to help her and Emmeline.

A French lady, Madame de Thoux, on the boat with her 12-year-old daughter, asks George about his home; she is interested in a slave who lived near there, George Harris. When George Shelby tells her the young man is married to his mother's servant Eliza and that both have escaped to Canada, Madame de Thoux tells him she is George Harris's sister, Emily. When Harris sold her to New Orleans, she was bought by a man who fell in love with her, took her to the West Indies, freed her, and married her; now she is a widow with a large inheritance and has come back to look for her brother. When George Shelby describes George Harris's wife, Eliza, Cassy realizes that Eliza is her own lost daughter.

Later, Cassy and Emmeline, together with Emily de Thoux, trace George and Eliza Harris to Montreal, where they have been living for five years and have had another child. The happy reunion soon changes Cassy into a devout Christian and a loving grandmother. George's sister wishes to share her inheritance with him and his family, and he accepts, saying he will use part of the money to educate himself. The whole family travels to France, where George attends a university for four years. Then, because of political upheavals in France, they return to the United States.

At this point, the narrator quotes from a long letter written by George Harris to a friend. George says that he would rather be darker-skinned than he is, for he feels more solidarity with the African race than with the white, and he wishes to cast his lot with them. He is hopeful that Liberia (which has been colonized by African Americans) will become a great, energetic republic, and he intends to go there. A few weeks later, George and his family go to Africa. The narrator tells us that Topsy, too, having grown up in New England with Ophelia and her family and having become a Christian, immigrated to Africa—as a missionary.

In Chapter XLIV, George Shelby returns home and tells Tom's wife that her husband is dead; as he promised Tom, he does not tell her the details of how he died. A month after returning, George gives each of his and his mother's slaves a certificate of freedom. George tells them, too, to remember Tom; it was at Tom's grave, he says, that he resolved never to own another slave.

In the last chapter of the book, the narrator (now in the person of Stowe herself) addresses readers directly, assuring them that most of the separate incidents and characters in the story are authentic; explaining that the passing of the Fugitive Slave Act of 1850 and its consequences made her determined to exhibit slavery "dramatically" in fiction; and exhorting all Americans, in all parts of the country, to do what they can to end slavery: to act directly and individually and above all to pray. Finally, she speaks directly to white Christians, saying they have much to answer for and reminding them that the millennium (with its implied promise of Christ's return) is near. If Christians do not follow the spirit of Christ, in regard to slavery, they will have to suffer God's wrath.

Commentary

Style & Language

The Gothic aspect of this book has been apparent during the last large group of chapters (from XXXII—"Dark Places"—forward), present in a number of details: the labyrinthine road through cypress swamps and pine forests; the ruined mansion; the mysterious, sexually powerful, and apparently mad "dark lady" (Cassy); and especially the monstrous Simon Legree, whom Cassy identifies metaphorically, at the end of Chapter XXXVI, as a vampire. Even Eva's death, in an earlier chapter, may be seen as an element typically Gothic in its nature (the wasting death of a fair virgin) if not in its character. Now, after Tom's "victory" (over Legree's attempted objectification, and over his own struggle not to allow himself to hate Legree) and his holy death, the Gothic aspect is indeed turned on its head (as critics Gilbert and Gubar have suggested). The "madwoman in the attic" becomes one of the chief "ghosts" haunting this house, and her success in frightening Legree—into allowing her and Emmeline's escape and into drinking himself to death—is grimly comic, especially in the tongue-in-cheek telling of it by Stowe's narrator.

But the deeper irony is that Legree's house *is* "haunted"—by the ghosts of all Legree's victims, by the ghosts of Cassy's children and Emmeline's mother, by Cassy herself as the ghost of the hopeful, trusting young girl she was long ago. These ghosts will remain in the house after Cassy and Emmeline have glided away in their sheets, and Legree's ghost, after the man's dreadful death, will join them. For these are all the spirits of slavery, rooted in greed, manifest in the use and objectification of human beings by other human beings and antithetical to Christian love. And Legree's decaying mansion, set among cotton fields and swamps, fallen down by now but not yet disappeared, is symbolic of the civilization these spirits will continue to haunt.

In tying the end of the novel to its beginning, Stowe perhaps strains our credulity a little by arranging for George Harris's sister to be traveling on the same river boat with George Shelby and Cassy. Still, the endings of sentimental novels traditionally abound with coincidences, and this one allows for such a happy reunion of family members that we would probably be small-minded to object to it—especially as the more realistic alternative would be to have Cassy and Emmeline travel on, never learning that Cassy's daughter Elise was really Eliza. (And that alternative may suggest to us how many former slaves must have traveled about the country, before and after the Civil War, looking in vain for brothers or sisters, mothers or children, sometimes perhaps sharing a road or a riverboat with someone else who—if either of them had known—was well acquainted with their lost one.) Most of the loose ends of the novel get tied up in these last chapters, although we are left to wonder, if we care to, about some of the many characters, such as Adolph and Rosa. This *is* probably realistic; Adolph will no longer be "Mr. St. Clare," but will bear the name of the young dandy who bought him.

George's immigration to Liberia was a point with which many early critics (who were in general more concerned with the social and political import of the book than its formal or aesthetic elements) found fault. Although Stowe's father, Lyman Beecher, was an advocate of "colonization" (like the fictional father of St. Clare's cousin Ophelia), it seems clear that Stowe herself was not a "colonizationist" but held opinions more in line in this regard with those expressed by St. Clare: How can one object to slavery as a wrong, she might have asked, and at the same time reject the slaves and former slaves themselves, urging them to go back to Africa, when most of them had never come from there in the first place. But Stowe *did* believe, apparently, that Africa was going to produce a "great civilization"—one of the wondrous events that would issue in the millennium, which was in the nineteenth century just close enough and at the same time just far enough away for people to predict all kinds of marvelous things about it. Some years after *Uncle Tom's Cabin* was published, however, Stowe admitted that, had she the last chapters to write over again, she would not send George and Eliza to Africa.

Style & Language

The final chapter—"Concluding Remarks"—was not part of the novel as originally serialized, nor does it appear in all editions since then. This chapter reflects Stowe's strong rhetorical schooling. First, she presents persuasive evidence (directed at 1852 readers and often addressed to specific pro-slavery arguments that were current then) not only that the incidents of her book were true in essence but also that freed slaves were indeed capable of being model citizens and supporting themselves and their families. Second, Stowe writes directly and eloquently to her readers as individuals, making each of them feel his or her direct responsibility for acting to end slavery—and, especially, making each feel that he or she *can* make a positive difference.

Glossary

"The sheeted dead . . . in the streets of Rome" William Shakespeare, *Hamlet*, I, 1: "In the most high and palmy state of Rome, / A little ere the mightiest Julius fell, / The graves stood tenantless and the sheeted dead / Did squeak and gibber in the Roman streets."

Elysium in Greek mythology, the dwelling place of virtuous people after death; by extension, any place or condition of ideal bliss or complete happiness; paradise.

CHARACTER ANALYSES

Uncle Tom

Tom is undeniably the central character of the novel that bears his name. He is of absolute importance to the major plot; he is the embodiment of the struggle that carries the major theme (the impact of slavery on human morality—or, to state it in more universal terms, the problem of evil as it threatens the human spirit). Tom is *not* a developing character in the usual sense—he experiences hope and joy, pain and despair, but he does not really change. He is in no way a better or a wiser or a different person at the end of the novel than he is at the beginning. Yet Tom is real and believable, and above all he is not the "Uncle Tom" of the twenty-first-century dictionary definition, the "elderly slave" who behaves "fawningly" towards whites.

Tom is described, early in the book, as a physically powerful man, very dark-skinned, with African features. We can calculate his age approximately: He is eight years older than Shelby, both he and Shelby are the fathers of sons in their early teens; thus he must be, when the book opens, somewhere in his middle 40s—still in the prime of life. Although some of Stowe's African-American characters are of racially mixed ancestry—almost always, it seems, for a specific reason related to plot or theme—Tom, although apparently born in the United States, is said to be "truly African," and this is also for a reason: Stowe believed that specific psychological characteristics were peculiar to people of different races or ethnicities—for example, that Italians were volatile and excitable, "Anglo-Saxons" aggressive and adventurous, "Irishmen" (and women) overly sentimental and quick to anger or tears. She believed that members of the "African race" were more gentle, more loving and devoted to family (and thus potentially better Christians) than whites, especially those she called "Anglo-Saxons." Thus we feel that she intended Tom's unmixed African blood to show these traits in his character. Her narrator also says of Tom, several times, that he is "childlike" and "simple"; she does not mean that he is intellectually slow, but that he is what we would call entirely *focused*, unburdened by complexities of motive or doubt, confident (Stowe would say) of the goodness of God.

In order to understand this simplicity and confidence in Tom's character, it is necessary to understand something of the Christianity in which Stowe herself was so firmly rooted. Traditional Calvinism, the religion of Stowe's childhood, holds that the "elect"—those whom God has chosen to be saved—can do nothing of their own will to change their chosen status, nor can those who are not among the elect do anything to change *their* situation. A person's actions *show* in which group he or she belongs. Stowe apparently did not subscribe completely to this theory; the "election" of many of her characters (Augustine St. Clare, for example) appears to be up for grabs, something to be settled, if not by the person's own good or evil deeds, then at least by prayer while the person is still alive. But Tom himself is obviously among the elect; this is shown by his bearing and his spiritual power for good upon others as well as by his own confidence and in the specific signs of grace that he receives—for example, the vision of Christ he experiences when tempted to despair on Legree's plantation. His election makes Tom a very strong character, but it also ensures that he will not change, as people like Cassy, St. Clare, even Legree change when Tom touches them.

Finally, it is important to recognize that Tom's passivity is not a character flaw, not a failure to act when he ought to act, but really a *kind of action*, a species of resistance and of what our century would call "existential choice." With each of his masters, from Shelby to Legree, Tom is pitted against materialism, which is the basis of slavery. Even in its most benign form, as manifested in St. Clare, this materialism denies the spiritual, denies human love, turns every human connection or virtue into something to be used for profit—the "making" of money (which is not really *made* but is extracted from the bodies and souls of those who are turned into things for this purpose).

Stowe's original subtitle for *Uncle Tom's Cabin* was "The Man Who was a Thing"; she meant it ironically, of course, because Tom refuses to be made a "thing." His inaction is this refusal; his passivity is love—not *liking*, for he does not like Legree and does not pretend to; not *admiration* or *attraction*, for Tom like the rest of us cannot freely give or withhold these things; but *love* in the sense that the New Testament defines it: "Love bears all things, believes all things, hopes all things, endures all things" (see *I Corinthians*, 13: 1–13). Love is the recognition of the human spirit in one human being by another human being; it is the antithesis of materialism and of slavery. Tom's courage, his strength, and his heroism are all based in the Christian love—the *good*— that he freely chooses (as, he believes, God freely chooses him) throughout the book.

Eliza

Eliza is the central figure in one of the two major plots, which she sets in motion by running away. She is the first example of a mother whose young child is sold, and she turns out—ironically—to be the only example of a child returned almost miraculously to a mother. She has what is probably the most famous scene in American literature when she leaps across the breaking ice on the Ohio; and she has a sweetly funny line when she disguises herself as a man and offers to "stamp and look saucy" in order to help with the illusion (George discourages this). But apart from these few things, and despite Stowe's assurances that her character was drawn from life, Eliza is a stock character, an abstraction—just another pretty face. Partly, this may have been to ensure that to white readers could identify with a young woman who looked and behaved in fashionable ways; partly, no doubt, Eliza's character as a conventionally "good" young woman was simply less interesting to Stowe than someone, for example, like Marie St. Clare.

But one possible reason that there seems to be little to say about Eliza, beyond the fact that she is conventionally good, is that she *was* drawn from life. Cassy tells Tom that Eliza was a timid, obedient child. Traumatized early by being sold away from her mother as a slave, then taken to Kentucky and given to young Mrs. Shelby, Eliza no doubt transferred her affection as much as possible to her new mistress and did what she could to please this very conventional and kind but passionless woman, becoming as much like Mrs. Shelby as possible.

George Harris

George Harris, Eliza's husband, quickly takes over Eliza's plot almost totally—partly because Eliza (unlike Chloe) is so traditionally submissive a wife that, had George been present when Haley caught up with her at the Ohio River, she might have fainted and allowed her husband to carry both her and Harry across; but also, partly, because George (like Chloe) has such a healthy sense of his own worth that he demands centrality. We like George from the moment that he tells Eliza, in the third chapter, that he is a better man than the one whose "property" he is. George manages to be incensed and indignant without being either sullen or arrogant; handsome, intelligent people who have been loved but not spoiled in their childhood seem to be able to pull this off, and George—although his stupid master treats him worse than badly—has been lucky enough to have an older sister who raised him well (before she disappeared into the fleshpots of New Orleans); an employer who saw him as a talented human being, rather than as a tool for making a larger profit; and of course a wife who worships him.

George's ancestry is mostly white, and we feel that Stowe consciously arranged this not only so that he could have a better chance of escaping (a bit of historically accurate unfairness) but also because his "Anglo-Saxon" blood, as she believed, allowed him to be more aggressive and adventurous than someone genetically closer to Africa. George himself, however, renounces his white ancestors in the end, saying he would prefer to have darker skin; obviously, he expects the great civilization that he (like Stowe) believes will make itself known in Africa to rise with or without the help of light-skinned people like himself. We readers (who no longer are tempted to ascribe his revolutionary zeal to any specific part of his genetic inheritance) may wish George well in the Liberia of his future, but perhaps the picture of him we find most memorable is that taken in the moment when he shouts defiance down to Loker, Marks, and their drunken posse—a speech definitely wasted upon such ears—and then shoots Loker, scaring the rest of them away.

Simon Legree

If Tom is the book's Christ-figure and George Harris its revolutionary Romantic hero, Simon Legree is without a doubt its anti-Christ, its arch-villain, or—as Cassy describes him—its vampire. If Tom's bearing and behavior show that he is among the elect, Legree's show quite definitely that he is not.

In several ways, as a character, Legree is indeed Tom's antithesis. We know nothing of Tom's past except that, as Shelby tells Haley in the first scene, he "got religion" at a camp meeting four years before the book opens. Of Legree we are told that, after he had spent some years at sea living a dissolute life, he was "almost persuaded" by his mother's prayers to reform but instead chose sin. (In both cases, according to traditional Calvinist doctrine, the apparent choice was really only an outward sign of the condition of the men's souls; however, Stowe's narrator describes Legree's critical moment as a genuine conflict between good and evil in which evil triumphs—just as, in Tom's moment of near despair, love and hope win the "victory.")

Now, whereas everyone whose life Tom touches is lifted and helped, Legree affects everyone near him for the worse. He has no family, only the artificial and perverse "family" he forces his slaves to enact: Cassy his "wife," whom he has used until nearly all of her actions (except those inspired by Tom) are hateful *re*actions against Legree; Emmeline his "daughter" whom he stole from her own mother and now wishes to force into an incestuous relationship (the nature of which Cassy senses, in her protection of the girl); Sambo and Quimbo his "brothers" (or "sons"), whom he uses as companions and henchmen, alternately punishes and rewards, and has turned into tools for draining the life and dignity from the field workers.

Like all of Tom's owners and like the book's other profiteers from the business of slavery, Legree is a materialist who sees human beings as nothing but material that can be used for profit. Like them all, with his reduction of slaves to the status of things, he has necessarily reduced himself to the same status—for part of what this book teaches is that to objectify others is to objectify oneself. But whereas Haley—probably genuinely—sees the nature of what he does only dimly (he has lied to himself successfully for so long that he believes he truly is a "man of humanity"), and whereas both Augustine St. Clare and Tom Loker, in different ways, are still capable of the "change of heart" that might save them (although in St. Clare's case it saves no one *but* him), Legree not only sees clearly what he is and what he does to others but also revels in it. He may tell the men in the riverboat bar that he uses slaves up and buys new ones for economic reasons, and he may pretend to Cassy (and even at times to himself) that he is concerned to keep Tom more or less healthy, or at least alive, in order to realize Tom's cost to him. But in truth, what he really wants is to exercise the absolute power of life and death—and more, the power of moral destruction—over these people.

Just as Legree uses alcohol "cautiously," so he exercises his power over his slaves as cautiously as he can, knowing that his real impulse is to go too far—for he hungers, perhaps even literally, for their blood. He reveals what he truly is in his jealousy of Tom, whose power to give hope and humanity to the other slaves cannot hurt Legree economically. What Legree wants, finally, is worship and fear; he has gone beyond capitalism and the profit motive and come out the other side.

Augustine St. Clare

Augustine St. Clare, Tom's third owner and the father of the novel's saintly child, is an odd and interesting character, an amalgam of traits that we finally find coherent and human. He is a "Byronic" hero, a thoughtful spokesman against slavery, and a reluctant (and at last repentant) materialist.

St. Clare's character contains a huge contradiction, in that he is a slaveowner whose way of life is sustained by the system he rejects morally and philosophically. This contradiction must somehow be explained, if we are to find him anything but a complete hypocrite, and Stowe explains it by showing him as a lazy man—physically and especially morally. This is understood to be a result of a traumatic experience in St. Clare's past: His heart was broken. If he had married his true love, it is implied, he would have lived in the North and opposed slavery more truly and effectively than his cousins, for he grew up with the system and hated it personally. But, alas, St. Clare was cheated and betrayed; he foolishly married Marie, who could probably not breathe without the help of slaves; and he begat little Eva, the image of his sainted mother and the light of his life. Thus, he has become cynical, knowing what is right but careless of the state of his own soul. His obligation to Eva keeps him from becoming entirely dissolute, and his moral despair allows him to live with the guilt of enjoying a comfortable life that is supported by owning slaves.

St. Clare also has the ironic self-knowledge that allows him to speak honestly against slavery despite being unable to reject its comforts for himself; he is like a principled vegetarian who, despite alternate amusement and self-loathing, cannot give up eating meat. His long conversations with Ophelia express many facets of the abolitionist arguments of Stowe's time, including Stowe's own disgust with the hypocrisy of the churches—which, St. Clare says, provide scriptural support for slavery because it is economically profitable, but would provide scriptural opposition to it if it suddenly became *un*profitable. But St. Clare's personal opposition to the system that provides him and his family with a comfortable, not to say luxurious, life has itself more than a whiff of hypocrisy, with which St. Clare seems generally unconcerned—until first Eva and then Tom are able to shake his complacency. St. Clare has been satisfied with avoiding sins of *commission* but has not recognized, until very late in his life, that sins of *omission* are as deadly. He does recognize this at last, and he fully intends to right his wrongs—soon, any day now. Ironically, although his intention and Tom's prayers are apparently enough to gain entrance to heaven for St. Clare in the end, his habits of idleness and materialism (habits instilled by the practice of slavery) have doomed the slaves he ought to have freed, including Tom, to a living hell.

Only one is saved. Because Ophelia insists on having legal control of Topsy, this child alone avoids the general sale of slaves when St. Clare dies and Marie inherits his property.

Topsy

Topsy shares the honors with Uncle Tom, Little Eva, and Eliza (crossing the ice) as one of the book's headline characters, always pictured on early cover illustrations, pigeon-toed and googly-eyed, with her hair sticking up in a million pigtails, next to blonde and angelic Eva—the archetypal "pickaninny" standing beside the archetypal little white girl. Her line to Ophelia, "S'pect I grow'd" (in answer to the question, "Do you know who made you?") was itself for a long time the basis of a common saying: "[G]rowed like Topsy" became a humorous way of describing how something developed without any particular intention or plan. In the book itself, Topsy is hardly a major character on a par with Tom, George, Legree, or even St. Clare, but neither is she comic relief. Like Chloe, she is a real person whom Stowe sketched expertly in a very few lines, whom we care about because, apparently, Stowe cared about her. Unlike Chloe, Topsy is someone who has been so battered by slavery that she might almost have been called, with some justification, "The Child Who was a Thing."

Topsy enters the book filthy, bruised, and scarred, dressed in a gunny sack, eight or so years old, and saved from a life as a tavern scullion by St. Clare, who sees her as a sort of gentle way of chiding Ophelia; his cousin "loves" slaves in theory but recoils from them in the flesh, and she preaches education for them without consideration of what this might entail. Let us see, St. Clare seems to think, what she will do with this very real child. And Topsy *is* a very real child, terribly abused but with enough resiliency to be good-natured despite her "depravity" (as Ophelia terms it; she lies, steals, gets out of tasks by throwing the materials for performing them away, leads the other children—except of course for Eva—into creative mischief), and with enough innate intelligence to be a very quick study when she wants to be. She is what our age would call a "survivor"—a little girl who will manage, with any luck at all, to land on her feet at all times.

Topsy is also an example of what happens when human beings are treated as commodities. Her parents were breeding stock, no more or less, and she was raised on a farm like a herd animal, not knowing who her mother was or, probably, that she even *had* a mother, taught absolutely nothing that she could not learn from her own observation. Her only use (since she is not light-skinned and thus potentially "beautiful" to white men, and since she is not yet old enough to be worth much as breeding stock herself) is as physical labor. The couple from whom St. Clare got her obtained her, no doubt, at a bargain price, and had he not bought her to teach Ophelia a lesson (and, to be fair to St. Clare, to rescue Topsy from being beaten with a stove poker), she would have grown up knowing nothing but what she could find out in their service. Since children are more energetic and stronger than adults, she would probably have been resold at puberty (or traded in for a younger model). By 25 or 30, on a sugar or cotton plantation like Legree's, she would have been used up, broken down and toothless and utterly worthless, and finally (but probably not quickly enough for Topsy) dead. Physical and psychological resiliency is of value in people used as things; brains are not, especially in females who will never be expected to carry on a cultivated conversation or add a column of figures.

The physical abuse Topsy has endured is awful; the mental abuse—an absolute lack of expectation for her development—is worse; and worst of all is the spiritual abuse. Only Eva and Ophelia see Topsy as a child of God, and only Eva (at first) sees her as lovable. Topsy herself knows nothing of love—to her, the word literally describes how she feels about candy, nothing more. She has never been loved, she has never loved, she does not love herself. This is the real crime committed against Topsy, and it is (as Stowe allows Topsy to show) the crime that slavery commits upon humanity—not only slaves but all of those who participate in or support it: the subordination of love to profit. To show an adult who despises herself will, unless she truly is despicable, at best puzzle readers; to show a child who does will arouse the sympathy of all but the most hard-hearted. The guilt that Topsy must have aroused in readers goes far toward explaining why her character was reduced, in white American myth, to a figure of fun.

CRITICAL ESSAYS

Themes in *Uncle Tom's Cabin*

In her work *"Uncle Tom's Cabin": Evil, Affliction and Redemptive Love*, critic Josephine Donovan says that the main theme of *Uncle Tom's Cabin* is "the problem of evil [shown on] several levels: theological, moral, economic, political, and practical." Almost certainly, Harriet Beecher Stowe, in writing the novel, set out to show not "the problem of evil" but the problem of a *specific* evil: the enslavement and use of human beings as the property of other human beings. In order to accomplish this goal in an effectively dramatic fashion, she could not merely present slavery as a monstrous wrong, chewing people up and spitting out what remained of them, physically and spiritually; she had to show it *in conflict with* a force that she knew to be more than equally powerful: the love of Christ. The theme of the novel then (not a simple theme, either, because of the levels Donovan enumerates) is this conflict.

Slavery is a powerful wrong. It is *said* to be wrong—in all cases, notwithstanding fair individual treatment of slaves—throughout the novel, first by George Harris, later and at length by Augustine St. Clare, and always by the narrator, directly as well as indirectly through the use of irony. It is *shown* to be wrong from the beginning of the book, despite the relatively benign setting of Shelby's Kentucky farm; again, individual slaves in individual cases may be well treated and even happy in their situations (as Eliza apparently has been), but the institution not only allows but is entirely based on the objectification of *all* slaves as commodities. Such objectification is evil, in the kind of actions it permits and supports and in the spiritual damage it does to individuals.

Because Shelby, portrayed as a decent if somewhat shallow and thoughtless man, is in debt, he is *forced*—according to law, because he owns property—to sell some of that property. The fact that he is also selling, as Chloe says, "heart's blood, heart's love," is, by that law, irrelevant. Shelby and Haley are introduced as a pair of opposites, one a "gentleman," the other a crass materialist of no sensitivity or cultivation. In fact, their participation in slavery makes them (as Haley reminds young George Shelby) the same. Haley sees all slaves, all the time, not as people but as profit or loss. Shelby sees them as such only when he is in serious money trouble, but this is a difference of degree, not kind. Shelby's selling of Eliza's child is, as an *act*, no less evil than Haley's selling of Lucy's baby to a passenger on the Ohio riverboat, although the consequences are quite different. Shelby tells Haley that he will not consider selling Eliza into sexual slavery (not because he knows this would be wrong, but because his wife would never forgive him), but he scarcely hesitates to sell little Harry into what he knows is almost surely the same fate.

Throughout the novel, Stowe shows slavery as hurtful and harmful to individual slaves, physically and emotionally; she knows this will have a wrenching emotional effect upon her audience. Thus Harris's forcing George to kill his own dog, Eliza's painful and frightened flight away from the only home she remembers, Tom's heartbroken farewell to his wife and children, the separation of old Aunt Hagar from her last and only child, the brutal whippings endured by George, Prue, Tom—all of these incidents are effective in showing the institution as it creates pain.

But even more terrible, from Stowe's point of view, is its creation of moral injury. Beginning subtly, with her sketch of Black Sam on Shelby's farm, whose morality is compromised by his need to promote himself as a favorite to his master (making him willing to help capture Eliza and her son if need be), Stowe shows slaves whose moral and spiritual soundness is damaged or destroyed by what happens to them. Lucy, on the steamboat, commits suicide despite Tom's efforts to help her. Old Prue, in New Orleans, tells Tom she would rather go to hell than to a heaven where white people are; she is in despair, and she dies in this condition. Cassy, too, is in despair; she has committed murder and attempted murder, and she is ready to kill Legree. St. Clare's slaves, who have learned to see themselves as materialistically as their owners see them, are morally degenerate. The thousands of slaves sold into sexual slavery or used sexually by their owners are in grave moral danger. Children like Topsy, raised to think of themselves as objects, of no value, are being set up, through absolutely no fault of their own, for morally barren lives—and worse, for lives of sin: the choice of evil over good.

Modern readers, who may have relatively little awareness of or respect for moral and spiritual matters, in comparison with matters physical and emotional, are apt to see these dangers as less important than they seemed to Stowe and her nineteenth-century audience. But to Stowe, the moral impact of slavery was among its chief evils, and to object that the moral responsibility belonged to the masters, not the slaves—who after all could not help themselves—would be a way of saying that these slaves were *not* adult human beings, people whose moral choices were their own to make. Yes, Stowe would agree that the masters were to blame for giving them nothing but difficult choices; but the moral choice for any action (or inaction) is made, she would say, by the person himself or herself. Slavery is evil because it attempts to reduce to objects *people who cannot be so reduced.*

The slaves themselves, of course, are not the only people whom slavery attempts to reduce and whom it thereby injures. The most obvious example of a slave *owner* destroyed by the institution is Marie St. Clare, whose narcissism is a result of her having been raised from infancy to believe that she is a superior kind of being. Marie's sadism is a natural result of her condition, as is her unhappiness: "If these people are not *real*, as *I* am *real*," Marie tells herself on one level, "then I may hurt them without guilt." But at the same time, she *knows* they are as real as she is—or that she is as unreal as they are—and this self-contradictory knowledge is the source of the imaginary pain she does feel and the very real pain she cannot. According to Stowe's lights, Marie is as doomed as Legree to a hell after death; meanwhile, she is in a kind of hell on earth—a different one from the one she subjects her slaves to, but a hell nonetheless. St. Clare himself, despite his role as one of the novel's chief spokesmen against slavery, has been morally injured by it; having found it easier to accept the institution than to combat it, he rejects spirituality for both his slaves and himself. Shelby and his wife are both shallow, callous people—as they must be if they are to continue owning slaves. At the physical center of the novel is St. Clare's nephew, the 12-year-old Henrique, shown to be potentially a kind, loving human being, who is being carefully trained and educated to be as meaningless to himself as Topsy, as soulless as Marie. Even Legree, who as the personification of the institution is an almost inhuman villain, is someone whom slavery has allowed and encouraged to become truly evil, morally dead before he has died physically.

Only Tom loves Legree. This is the irony at the heart of the novel, the key to its thematic conflict. In order to understand what it means, we need to remember, first, that Legree personifies *slavery*, which is evil precisely because it reduces (or attempts to reduce) human beings to property—material objects devoid of spiritual existence and value. But slavery cannot *actually* objectify human beings; Christian love (Christ's love, from which, Tom says in his dying words, we are inseparable) is stronger. Tom is able to separate slavery from its personification in Legree, to "hate the sin but love the sinner." By being able to love Legree, to forgive him (a spiritual feat that is not easy even for Tom to achieve, one that he calls "a victory"), Tom is able to triumph over the evil that Legree personifies.

We need also to remember that Tom does not love Legree in the material sense (in which Topsy, for example, says she loves candy), nor yet in the emotional sense that Tom loves his children. He does not love him, as some readers have apparently thought, in the sense that a prisoner of war begins to "love" (really, to depend upon, to "identify with" in self-protection) his captors. Tom loves Legree as, according to the Gospel of Matthew (5: 44), Christ counseled his listeners to "love their enemies"; he forgives Legree as, according to the Gospel of Luke (23: 34), Christ as he died forgave the men who had crucified him. According to Christian doctrine, this kind of *love* is the respect due one's fellow human beings, not because they have earned it but because they are human beings. It is precisely the kind of love that slavery denies when it denies people their humanity and views them as objects, commodities to be bought and sold, property to be used in the gaining of profit.

The theme of *Uncle Tom's Cabin*, then, is the conflict between the evil of slavery and the *good* of Christian love. Eva, symbolic of this sort of love, is killed (mythically) by slavery, but like Tom, she triumphs over death and thus over evil. If Tom were willing to hate Legree, to deny him Christian love, still he would not necessarily be willing to kill the man, as Cassy asks, or to allow Cassy to kill him, or to run away along with Cassy and Emmeline and leave Legree's other slaves to face the consequences—nor, of course, would he necessarily be willing to give up Cassy and Emmeline's hiding place to Legree; the difference, however, would be one of degree, not of kind. Tom too, then, dies but triumphs over death—as, we are meant to understand, do the two men who have carried out Legree's orders to kill him, saved from evil by Tom's dying love and forgiveness. Legree does not so triumph; in spite of Tom's prayers, we are told that he continues to choose evil and at last dies in it, physically as he has spiritually—and no doubt luckily for the popularity of the novel, whose readers might have protested had the villain been allowed to escape his just punishment in the afterlife.

A Mosaic of Movement and Conflict

Much of the attention that readers and critics have given to *Uncle Tom's Cabin* has been directed to its content—the development of its themes, the significance of its characters and incidents. Increasingly, however, there has been focus on the book's *structure*, which is generally now recognized as strong and balanced. Above all, we can see ways in which that structure is effectively and integrally related to features of the novel's plot movements and thematic conflicts—including ironically revealing symmetries and juxtapositions of incident.

Stowe herself was aware of the relationship between her structural choices and her purposes. Although the manner of its initial publication (in serial form) was certainly a determining factor in the novel's episodic nature, Stowe knew that—in order to persuade readers actively to oppose slavery—she would have to touch their emotions. Thus she chose to write what she called "a series of *sketches*" (Stowe's emphasis;

quoted in Donovan's *"Uncle Tom's Cabin": Evil, Affliction, and Redemptive Love*). Having had considerable success in this popular literary form, Stowe must have felt confident with it; but she used the term *sketches* metaphorically as well in this case, for she went on to say "there is no arguing with *pictures*" (Donovan 30). Stowe had, in fact, been trained as a visual artist, and it is easy to see her eye for detail, color, movement and composition in her written work. She knew, too, that the reason "there is no arguing with pictures" has to do with the fact that people take in visual stimuli on a much more basic level than they do intellectual arguments; as much as possible, she wanted to hit her audience hard and directly at that level.

But if a "series of sketches" is a *linear* composition (as any conventional novel must to a great extent be), Stowe also thought of her composition in *Uncle Tom's Cabin* as an overall design. In another statement that compares the book to visual art, she said she thought of it as a "mosaic" of "stones" (Donovan 30), in which all the pieces (or "fragments") contribute to the overall whole. Stowe's comparison here is later echoed by critic Elaine Showalter in her essay "Piecing and Writing" (in *The Poetics of Gender*), who views the book's structure as similar to that of a patchwork quilt—fittingly, one made in the popular "Log Cabin" pattern. In both the mosaic design and the quilt images, we see parts, each with its own shape, color, and perhaps interior design, fitted together to make a larger piece of art. The effect is not linear but overall, and it includes the possibilities of balance, direction, and movement.

We can begin to see—literally—the sort of design that is present in *Uncle Tom's Cabin*, if we arrange the book's 45 chapters in a more-or-less symmetrical shape, using some arbitrary symbols to identify them: say, an X for each chapter in the "Eliza" plot, an O for each one in the "Tom" plot, and an 8 for each in which the two plots are combined. (Chapter XLV, "Concluding Remarks," not part of the original serial publication, can be a <> at the design's base.) Here it is:

8

XXO8XX

XXOXOX

OOOXOOO

OOOOOOOO

OOOOOOOO

XOOOOO8

O

<>

Although not exactly symmetrical, it is balanced, with the Eliza plot, thematically less weighty but more conventionally "exciting" to readers and certainly more cheerful (both important considerations in a work that aims at popularity), presented more often in the first third of the novel, while the Tom plot, appearing alone only three times in the first thirteen chapters, dominates the second two-thirds of the book. If our design were drawn in more detail—subdividing the two plots into large and small X's and O's to show, for example, the Quaker sections of the Eliza plot and the St. Clare sections of the Tom plot—we would see a more various pattern emerging. And if the X's and O's were in color, with brighter colors for the chapters in which the dominant moods were hopeful, darker ones for those in which despair and pain dominate, then—well, the reader may imagine that visual effect. It would be striking.

It would also show movement, as the arrangement marked changes from the quiet colors of the opening chapters to the brighter and brighter hues of Eliza and George's escape through the northern states into Canada, interspersed more frequently with the darkening colors of Tom's captivity as he travels first down the Ohio, then the Mississippi to New Orleans, and finally up the Red River in Louisiana to Simon Legree's plantation. As both plots move, so does the novel's structure, although first the Tom plot and then the Eliza plot are delayed, time-wise, in order for each plot's chapters to be arranged most effectively in terms of the overall design.

If there were also some way to show, in our design, degrees of *conflict* within the chapters, both the complexity of the overall picture and of the patterns of movement within it would be further enhanced. Throughout her absorbing study of the novel, Josephine Donovan emphasizes its *dialectic* structure: the tension between such opposites as the Shelby farm (with Tom and Chloe's cabin and Shelby's great house themselves at its heart) and Legree's plantation, the northward escape of Eliza's family and Tom's southward journey, the cool organization of the Quaker farms and the hot chaos of the New Orleans household, the "heavenly" sanctuary of Canada and the hell of Legree's plantation. Within these greater tensions are dozens of lesser ones; in the St. Clare chapters alone, for example, we find, among other dialectical oppositions, those between Marie St. Clare and Cousin Ophelia, between St. Clare and his twin brother, between the cook Dinah and the "upstairs" servants. And over the whole "design" presented by the book are the great tensions between slavery and freedom, evil (materialism, the objectification of human beings) and good (self-realization, spirituality, Christian love).

Sometimes these dialectical oppositions are shown as actual conflict (as, for example, the physical conflict in Chapter XVII between George Harris and Tom Loker—or, in Chapter XXXVIII, the verbal conflict between Tom and Legree *and* the spiritual conflict within Tom himself). Sometimes the tension is simply presented without a great deal of comment or actual confrontation (as, for example, the ironic oppositions of "the cabin of the man" to "the halls of the master"—including the relationships of the people who inhabit both dwellings—on Shelby's farm). If we could, within our design, somehow depict these oppositions (conflicts, tensions) in their growth, their rising and falling, their resolutions (if any), we might see an even more various and intriguing pattern of composition and movement.

But within the patterns of movement, something else becomes apparent. As art teachers used to tell their students tirelessly, the *asymmetrical* elements of a design convey movement and interest, while the *symmetrical* ones, which need not be obvious, give strength and solidity. An examination of the chapter arrangement in *Uncle Tom's Cabin* reveals, beneath the conscious asymmetry, a symmetry of ironic juxtaposition that further enhances our understanding of the novel's structure.

First, we may notice that Chapters VII and XXXVIII, near the beginning and near the end of the book (at exactly the same respective distance from each, in fact, if "Concluding Remarks" is seen as an epilogue rather than an actual part of the novel) are oddly mirror-images of each other: in the first, Eliza is almost captured by Haley, but in desperation (and with the help of a miracle, according to Black Sam's eyewitness interpretation of the event) crosses the icy river to safe haven. In the second, Legree nearly pushes Tom over the brink of despair, but in a desperation described as "numb" (and with the help of a miracle—a vision of Jesus as he gazes at the dying fire), Tom gains a new and unremitting hold on his faith. The first of these chapters is entitled "The Mother's Struggle"; the second is "The Victory."

Two more events are similarly juxtaposed, both near the middle of the book: Prue's death at the beginning of Chapter XIX and Eva's at the end of Chapter XXVI. The death of little Eva was, for many nineteenth-century readers, the emotional heart of the novel, the sentimentalized scene of a "beautiful" death, with the dying child surrounded by the tears and prayers of those who love her. Set across from this, in what must be nearly the most unrelentingly bitter irony in literature, is the death of the old slave woman, beaten horribly and left alone in the cellar. (The reader who believes *Uncle Tom's Cabin* to be a children's book—

or its author to be a gentle sentimentalist—should re-read the passage in which this death is described.)

And at the very center of the book, in Chapter XXIII, juxtaposed in their own chapter by the reasonable argument of two men who then break off arguing to play a game of backgammon, are the two 12-year-old boys, Henrique and Dodo. One, the master, hits the other, the slave, in the face with his riding whip, knocks him down, and beats him. This is the only appearance of either of these characters in the novel, and their encounter is understated—yet its position in the book makes it literally of *central* importance. One wonders if the placing of this particular "fragment" was not a conscious decision by the mosaic artist.

Until the twentieth century, the design of a novel as basically *linear* was more or less taken for granted. That is, indeed, the sort of design first apparent to a reader whose acquaintance with any book is most likely to be based on *time* and *direction*, from beginning to end. But viewed at once, overall (as is possible after we have read the complete book), a novel's design may be startling and revealing. As Harriet Beecher Stowe herself suggested, and as other writers have since noted, *Uncle Tom's Cabin*'s structure works both in a linear way and as an overall pattern—a mosaic, a quilt—which may be examined visually in order to discover unexpected patterns of movement and opposition.

The Haunted Cabin: *Uncle Tom* and the Gothic

Numerous critics (including Helen Waite Papashvily in 1956 and Philip Fisher in 1985) have discussed *Uncle Tom's Cabin* as being in the tradition of fictional *sentimentalism*, a tradition that also includes many of the works of such nineteenth-century realists as Walter Scott and Maria Edgeworth, whom Stowe took as models. Other critics have suggested an element of the Gothic in Stowe's book; most notably, Sandra M. Gilbert and Susan Gubar, writing in 1979 (*The Madwoman in the Attic: The Woman Writer and the Nineteenth-Century Imagination*), see Cassy as an ironic example of a Gothic archetype, the "madwoman in the attic." And if the relationship between sentimentalism and the Gothic had never been otherwise noted, one could hardly escape it in this novel, where a real Gothic power lurks like a deep shadow behind its own ironic evocation in the closing chapters.

Sentimentalism can be recognized by the presence of various elements within a fictional work. One is the assumption that *heartfelt feeling* (often seen as a *feminine* attribute) is better, more trustworthy, than *intellect* or *reason*. Chapter IX ("In Which it Appears That a Senator Is but a Man") is only the most emphatic illustration of this assumption in the novel. Another such element is stress on the importance of morality; yet another is the presence of certain sentimental character types, of which—although no character in this novel is entirely stereotypical—George Harris (the "tamed" sentimental hero), Eliza (the innocent heroine), and St. Clare (the "Byronic" or untamed hero) are to a great extent examples. The primacy of marriage and the family, and the special importance of the relationship between mother and child, are also typical.

But sentimentalism and the Gothic are often closely linked, both historically and thematically, and almost all examples of Gothic literature have strong sentimental underpinnings. Moreover, while not all sentimentalist works have Gothic elements, many do—for example, the novels of Charles Dickens, which *Uncle Tom's Cabin* resembles in numerous ways. Among the elements that most frequently identify the Gothic in literature are themes of oppression and guilt (which are often characterized as being handed down through generations), inequality in power struggles (with, often, the feminine or "feminized" characters suffering in consequence of such struggles), and stereotypical Gothic characters (typical sentimental characters exaggerated: the innocent heroine becomes a helpless victim, the "tamed" hero is powerless to save her, the "untamed" hero—out of control, his "masculine" attributes of aggression and acquisitiveness unchecked—becomes the Gothic villain or monster). These elements, too, are present in Stowe's novel, as the reader will recognize—even the Gothic characters, although their relationships with each other are unconventional.

Also identifying the Gothic are a number of typical objects, characters, motifs, or incidents that writer Thomas Thornburg, in "The Quester and the Castle: A Study in the Gothic Novel with Special Emphasis on Bram Stoker's *Dracula*," has called "trappings" of the Gothic. Among the most familiar of these are the ruined mansion, the haunted house or castle, the lost or misdirected letter, the dark and winding road or labyrinth, the "wasteland" or barrens, nightmares (what Thornburg calls "Gothic dreams," including birth dreams), and, of course, the vampire. These "trappings" appear in abundance, especially from Chapter XXXI onward, and the title of Chapter XXXII ("Dark Places") suggest that Stowe consciously brought them in. Legree's unkempt house and yard, once beautiful, have fallen into ruin; the house is said to be haunted (by the ghost of an imprisoned slave,

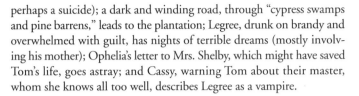

perhaps a suicide); a dark and winding road, through "cypress swamps and pine barrens," leads to the plantation; Legree, drunk on brandy and overwhelmed with guilt, has nights of terrible dreams (mostly involving his mother); Ophelia's letter to Mrs. Shelby, which might have saved Tom's life, goes astray; and Cassy, warning Tom about their master, whom she knows all too well, describes Legree as a vampire.

The Gothic elements virtually disappear after the novel's climax, at the beginning of Chapter XXXVIII ("The Victory"), when Tom's vision and his renewal of faith render even Legree harmless (harmless, that is, to Tom's soul); the villain stamps and curses, but he senses his own ineffectuality, and the "haunted house" scheme that Cassy cooks up is a parody of the Gothic. Ironically, only Legree is frightened now, and his bad dreams (helped along by the liquor he takes to dull them) quickly kill him—a horrible death, the narrator tells us, but one that she doesn't even glorify by describing. Still, while they dominate the chapters from XXXII through the beginning of XXXVIII, the Gothic elements are effective in deepening the spiritual darkness that confronts and threatens Tom. But serving the novel's atmosphere is not their only function.

Seeing *Uncle Tom's Cabin*, if not as a Gothic novel *per se*, then as a novel that shares in certain elements of the Gothic, may help us to understand some aspects of the book more clearly. Cassy, as Gilbert and Gubar point out, is indeed stereotypical in certain ways of a Gothic figure, the "dark woman" who is threatening to the hero and heroine either through her sexual appetites or her "madness," or both. The specific "dark woman" who Cassy brings to these readers' minds is Bertha Mason, Rochester's first wife in Emily Brontë's *Jane Eyre*. Bertha, a Creole woman from the West Indies, is violently insane, murderous (she frequently escapes from her tipsy keeper and tries to kill Rochester), and her insanity is said to result from her having inherited a family tendency (on her mother's side) to excess—alcoholism is stated, sexual excess is implied. In Jean Rhys's *Wide Sargasso Sea*, Bertha—here called Antoinette, the Brontë character's first name—is portrayed as a normal but troubled young woman whose brother arranges her marriage to Rochester. The sexual passion their union inspires frightens Rochester, as does almost everything about his bride's culture, and he takes her back to England and imprisons her. Like Cassy, Antoinette / Bertha is the victim of an economic system that uses her as an object (Rochester marries her for her dowry) and punishes her for her sexuality.

Cassy, of course, has been used sexually since her early teens. Like all the African and African-American slave girls and women sold for such use, she was not only less able to resist but was thought to be more sexually passionate than white women—sexual passion being, in sentimental / Gothic tradition, a "masculine" attribute which, in a woman, calls for punishment. Ironically, the use to which Cassy has been put has indeed driven her nearly mad (the same is true of Rhys's Antoinette), and Tom's first glimpse of her through a window in Legree's house is of that stereotypical "madwoman." But by the time she "haunts" the attic with Emmeline, Cassy has recovered her sanity with Tom's help, and her appearance as a Gothic figure now is only a parody of the stereotype.

The Gothic typically divides the sentimental heroine into two parts—one, the "dark woman" whose passions make her dangerous; the other, the "fair" woman (although of course these physical characteristics are not always adhered to) who is often portrayed as nearly sexless and whose attractions (to the hero, but also to the villain or monster) are those of a *victim*, arousing sadistic interest in the villain, the urge to protect in the hero (but these two are often more closely related to each other than either would like to admit). This "fair" Gothic woman is an exaggeration of the helpless, fluttery, and fainting sentimental heroine so fashionable in the late eighteenth and nineteenth centuries, and her death (or her near-death, if the sentimental plot is stronger than the Gothic) is an almost obligatory scene in Gothic novels from *The Castle of Otranto* to *Dracula*. There is, of course, such a character in *Uncle Tom's Cabin*: it is Eva, the little girl whose death dominated early dramatic productions based (often very loosely) on the novel.

Eva is certainly not a standard Gothic "fair" heroine, nor is her death brought about (as it ought typically to be) by the Gothic villain of the book, Simon Legree, who does not even appear until after Eva has died. But Eva's presence here, and her dying, are unmistakable signs of the Gothic nature of the book. Critics have noted Eva's resemblance to the frail, oddly sexless, Gothic "fair woman," and readers have questioned the meaning of her death, which is obviously a central incident in the novel. Eva dies of tuberculosis (although the name of the disease is never mentioned), but *mythically*, it is slavery itself that kills her. For slavery itself is the monster, created by materialism and the profit motive, that towers over everything in *Uncle Tom's Cabin*.

Simon Legree is one of slavery's embodiments (as, to a lesser degree, are Shelby, Haley, St. Clare, and indeed every white person who refuses or declines to oppose slavery). Legree is, metaphorically and mythically at least, a vampire: Cassy tells Tom that Legree will dog him and have his blood, as indeed Legree eventually does, through the agency of his two overseers. The other slaveowners are vampires as well, achieving their own "life" ("making their living") through slaves whose lives they use. The vampire in literature—from John Polidori's malicious and thinly disguised portrait of Byron in "The Vampyre" to the mysterious monster of Stephen King's '*Salem's Lot*—has long been associated with the power of money and class oppression. The most famous of all literary vampires, Bram Stoker's Dracula, is a nobleman who drinks the blood of his own feudal serfs and uses wealth to gain entrance to England. Stowe's novel was published almost 50 years before Stoker's, and she probably had not read Karl Marx on capitalism, but Cassy's metaphor of the profiteer as bloodsucker seems to have been in the nineteenth-century air.

If *Uncle Tom's Cabin* is a sentimentalist novel, it is certainly also reflective of that inevitable sentimental reflection, the Gothic. In its characters, incidents, themes, and various "trappings," Harriet Beecher Stowe's famous book displays dark Gothic features whose examination may shed new light on this American classic.

CliffsNotes Review

Use this CliffsNotes Review to test your understanding of the original text and reinforce what you've learned in this book. After you work through the review and essay questions, identify the quote section, and the fun and useful practice projects, you're well on your way to understanding a comprehensive and meaningful interpretation of *Uncle Tom's Cabin*.

Q&A

1. Tom's first owner, Mr. Shelby, sells Tom because

   a. Shelby believes slavery is wrong and wants to get out of it

   b. Shelby is deeply in debt and is being pressed for payment

   c. Shelby is offended by Tom's practice of Christianity

2. George Harris, Eliza's husband, has

   a. invented a machine for cleaning hemp

   b. knocked his owner into the mill pond

   c. married another woman, on his owner's orders

3. Little Eva, Augustine and Marie St. Clare's daughter, dies from

   a. an "insidious disease" (tuberculosis) that is never named in the book

   b. injuries suffered in a riding accident at the St. Clare summer estate

   c. food poisoning, for which Marie has her cook whipped to death

4. Topsy, the little girl St. Clare buys for his cousin Ophelia to educate, had been raised

   a. on Simon Legree's plantation, cared for by Cassy

   b. by a speculator

   c. in a New Orleans brothel, cared for by prostitutes

5. When Legree makes it clear that he will have Tom whipped to death if Tom does not reveal where Cassy and Emmeline are, Tom

   a. refuses to tell and is whipped to death

   b. makes up a story and then runs away

   c. resists until George Shelby arrives to save him

6. Cassy and Emmeline eventually get away from Legree's mansion by

   a. hiding in the swamps until Legree gives up the search

   b. walking out the front door dressed in sheets

   c. setting fire to the house and leaving in the confusion

   Answers: (1) b. (2) a. (3) a. (4) b. (5) a. (6) b.

Identify the Quote

1. Marcies! . . . don't see no marcy in't! 'taint right! . . . Mas'r never ought ter left it so . . . . Ye've arnt him all he gets for ye, twice over. He owed ye yer freedom, and ought ter gin't to yer years ago. Mebbe he can't help himself now, but I feel it's wrong . . . . Them as sells heart's love and heart's blood, to get out thar scrapes, de Lord'll be up to 'em!

2. Well, . . . suppose that something should bring down the price of cotton once and forever, and make the whole slave property a drug in the market, don't you think we should soon have another version of the Scripture doctrine? What a flood of light would pour into the church all at once, and how immediately it would be discovered that everything in the Bible and reason went the other way [i.e., against slavery].

3. I know very well that you've got the law on your side, and the power . . . . and your laws *will* bear you out in it, more shame for you and them! But you haven't got us. We don't own your laws; we don't own your country; we stand here as free, under God's sky, as you are; and, by the great God that made us, we'll fight for our liberty till we die.

4. Couldn't never be nothin' but a nigger, if I was ever so good . . . If I could be skinned, and come white, I'd try then.

   Answers: (1) Chloe speaking to Tom about Shelby, who has sold her husband; it is the morning Tom must be taken away by Haley, and Tom has tried to tell Chloe to forgive Shelby. (2) Augustine St. Clare talking to his wife, Marie, about the way the churches defend slavery by quoting Scripture to support it; he says if slavery were not economically good for them, they'd turn completely around and oppose it. (3) George Harris calling down from the rocks to Loker, Marks, two constables, and a posse below, who have pursued George and his party and intend to return them to slavery. (4) Topsy talking to Eva, who has just told Topsy that people would love her if she would try to be good; Topsy has been observant for long enough to see no point in trying.

Essay Questions

1. Tom has been brought up on charges in the court of public opinion, and you have been part of his defense team. Write a summation to the jury, defending Tom against the charge that he is an "Uncle Tom"—that is, "fawning and servile in his behavior to whites." Stress any points in Tom's experience, behavior, and / or philosophy that seem to you to be relevant in his defense.

2. Simon Legree has been charged with Tom's murder. You considered resigning from your law firm, which Legree hired to defend him, but your boss talked you out of it. Now you have been assigned to write a brief explaining why Legree should be convicted of a lesser charge. Write an essay in which you present any evidence and / or logical arguments you can find to support the idea that, considering Legree's culture and the circumstances surrounding Tom's death, Legree should not be charged with capital murder.

3. Compare and / or contrast any two characters in *Uncle Tom's Cabin* who seem to you to present an interesting opposition or likeness (for example, Chloe and Cassy, Mrs. Shelby and Marie St. Clare, Haley and Legree, Topsy and Eva, etc.). Focus on three or four points (character traits, important influences, effects on other characters, and so on) that seem to you especially characteristic of your choices.

4. Discuss how (or even whether) *Uncle Tom's Cabin* might be dramatized and presented in a modern production (in whole or in part) without offending modern audiences.

Practice Projects

1. Select a scene or group of scenes, of whatever combined length seems appropriate, given your time and resources, as the basis of a doll- or puppet-theater (or "claymation," or other figure-animation) dramatic presentation based on *Uncle Tom's Cabin*. Write a script, make or adapt figures of the characters, make costumes or sets if necessary, and produce a video of your scene or scenes. You may choose to follow Stowe's book and dialogue loosely or exactly. (This might be an interesting group project.)

2. Create a painting, collage, or other visual presentation based on *Uncle Tom's Cabin*. This could be a realistic, representational drawing or sketch of a scene, setting, character or characters, or an abstract composition (perhaps based on the book's structure—see "A Mosaic of Motion and Conflict" in the Critical Essays of this guide), or anything else that the novel suggests to you.

CliffsNotes Resource Center

The learning doesn't need to stop here. CliffsNotes Resource Center shows you the best of the best—links to the best information in print and online about the author and / or related works. And don't think that this is all we've prepared for you; we've put all kinds of pertinent information at www.cliffsnotes.com. Look for all the terrific resources at your favorite bookstore or local library and on the Internet. When you're online, make your first stop www.cliffsnotes.com where you'll find more incredibly useful information about *Uncle Tom's Cabin*.

Books

This CliffsNotes book provides a meaningful interpretation of *Uncle Tom's Cabin*. If you are looking for information about the author and / or related works, check out these other publications:

Uncle Tom's Cabin: Evil, Affliction, and Redemptive Love, by Josephine Donovan. This thoughtful, gracefully written study is very brief and succinct, with a section on the background, critical history, and importance of the work, and another giving a critical reading. There is a helpfully annotated bibliography. Boston: Twayne, 1991.

Uncle Tom's Cabin and American Culture, by Thomas F. Gossett. An excellent book for the general reader, this looks at the background of the novel, reactions to it in the U.S. and elsewhere, its relationship to American culture, and the dramatic presentations based upon it, from the 1850s to the 1980s. Dallas, TX: Southern Methodist University Press, 1985.

Harriet Beecher Stowe: A Life, by Joan D. Hedrick. The first new biography of Stowe in many years, Hedrick's authoritative, Pulitzer Prize-winning work is both scholarly and very readable. This is a big book in every sense, and well worth the time of any reader interested in *Uncle Tom's Cabin*, Stowe herself, and / or her culture and times. New York: Oxford University Press, 1994.

Africans in America: America's Journey Through Slavery, by Charles Johnson, Patricia Smith, and WGBH [Boston] Series Research Team. *Africans in America* is a companion book to the PBS series of the same name (produced by WGBH Boston), but it stands on its own as an excellent general overview of slavery—probably the best book of its kind. It includes narrative, excerpts from historical texts, twelve related fictional sketches by Charles Johnson, and many illustrations. New York: Harcourt, Brace, 1998.

The Building of Uncle Tom's Cabin, by E. Bruce Kirkham, is a thorough study of the background, composition, and publication of the novel. Josephine Donovan calls this "Probably the single most valuable secondary work on the novel for the scholar." Knoxville: University of Tennessee Press, 1977.

New Essays on Uncle Tom's Cabin, edited by Eric J. Sundquist, is a collection of critical essays on all aspects of the novel. Some of the essays are unfavorable, which will help to introduce readers to different viewpoints and to provide them with a realistic slant on late twentieth-century Stowe criticism. Cambridge, UK: Cambridge University Press, 1986.

It's easy to find books published by IDG Books Worldwide, Inc. You'll find them in your favorite bookstores (on the Internet and at a store near you). We also have three Web sites that you can use to read about all the books we publish:

■ www.cliffsnotes.com

■ www.dummies.com

■ www.idgbooks.com

Internet

Check out these Web resources for more information about Harriet Beecher Stowe and Uncle Tom's Cabin:

Key to Uncle Tom's Cabin—Chapter III, http://xroads. virginia.edu—Stowe published *The Key to Uncle Tom's Cabin* after the novel's unprecedented popularity had prompted Southern writers to claim that the novel was an abolitionist fabrication and that its incidents had no basis in reality. With the help of family and friends, Stowe collected documentary evidence to support the claims she had made about various aspects of slavery in the novel. Chapter III is representative. To access this page, at the American Studies at the University of Virginia home page. click the Search button and enter **Uncle Tom's Cabin** in the text box.

Classical Literature Library Home Page, www.selfknowledge.com—
Offers the complete online HTML text, extensively annotated, with
references cross-linked to the Encyclopedia of the Self. To access
Uncle Tom's Cabin, click the link to Harriet Beecher Stowe in the
author list.

Lecture Notes on Uncle Tom's Cabin, www.gonzaga.edu/faculty/
campbell/enl311/utc.htm—From the Gonzaga University
English Department, these insightful notes will be valuable to students and teachers.

Uncle Tom's Cabin: From newspaper to book to play to image,
http://info.berkeley.edu/courses/lis182/tom.html
This site includes links to fourteen illustrations—posters, handbills,
and a newspaper advertisement—in black / white and color, from
nineteenth- and early twentieth-century dramatic productions of
Uncle Tom's Cabin. Most are from the San Francisco Performing Arts
Library. The art is interesting, some of it beautiful, and the artists' con-
ceptions, in these years, of scenes and characters from the novel can
be enlightening.

Next time you're on the Internet, don't forget to drop by www.cliffs
notes.com. We created an online Resource Center that you can use today,
tomorrow, and beyond.

Magazines and Journals

Following are four articles that span a 20-year period during which the
meaning of Stowe's book in American history and culture was being reeval-
uated:

Ammons, Elizabeth. "Heroines in Uncle Tom's Cabin." American Literature 49, no. 2 (May 1977): 161–79. This article explores the importance of *Uncle Tom's Cabin* from a feminist viewpoint.

Brown, Gillian. "Getting in the Kitchen with Dinah: Domestic Politics in
Uncle Tom's Cabin." American Quarterly 36, no. 4 (Fall, 1984):
503–23. Like the Ammons' article, Brown's article also explore's
Stowe's novel from a feminist viewpoint.

Graham, Thomas. "Harriet Beecher Stowe and the Question of Race."
New England Quarterly 46, No. 4 (December 1973): 614–22. In
this article, Graham attempts to refute charges of racism leveled
against the novel and its author.

Send Us Your Favorite Tips

In your quest for knowledge, have you ever experienced that sublime moment when you figure out a trick that saves time or trouble? Perhaps you realized you were taking ten steps to accomplish something that could have taken two. Or you found a little-known workaround that achieved great results. If you've discovered a useful resource that gave you insight into or helped you understand *Uncle Tom's Cabin* and you'd like to share it, the CliffsNotes staff would love to hear from you. Go to our Web site at www.cliffsnotes.com and click the Talk to Us button. If we select your tip, we may publish it as part of CliffsNotes Daily, our exciting, free e-mail newsletter. To find out more or to subscribe to a newsletter, go to www.cliffsnotes.com on the Web.

Index